P9-CDD-874

P R A I S E   F O R
MANAGERS AS MENTORS

"Chip Bell has done it again. This tightly written, straight from the shoulder book brings helpful techniques to any manager who would be a mentor."

> —James A. Autry, author of *Confessions of an Accidental Businessman* and *Love and Profit*

"The book managers everywhere have been waiting for: a clear and practical guide to tapping the talent in their organizations. If you ever wondered what managers in 'learning organizations' are supposed to be doing, here's your answer."

> —Nancy K. Austin, coauthor of *A Passion for Excellence*

"The concept of Chip Bell's brilliance is that every leader must become a mentor to his or her employees. Buy the book and find out how."

> —Jeffrey Gitomer, Syndicated Columnist, "Sales Moves"

"*Managers As Mentors* opens new vistas to managers and leaders who are broadening and deepening their skills as developers of human talent—an essential element of success in business today."

> —Todd Clist, Executive Vice President, Marriott Lodging

Winner of the *Mentor Newsletter*
1997 ATHENA AWARD
for Excellence in Mentoring

"**C**hip Bell beautifully teaches techniques for developing a true partnership and clearly illustrates the real organizational power of mentoring."

—Sandy West, Executive Vice President, Victoria's Secret

"**M**anaging through mentoring is a 'must' skill for successful managers. Chip Bell offers an in-depth, step-by-step study of how to acquire and practice this creative art."

—Jim Miller, CEO, Miller Business Systems and author of *The Corporate Coach*

"*Managers As Mentors* suggests that managers need to assume the role of mentor for their own direct reports. Bell outlines simple, easy-to-follow steps so that the mentoring role becomes comfortable and doable—even for the busiest managers."

—Dr. Beverly Kaye, coauthor of *Designing Career Development Systems*

"*Managers As Mentors* offers deep insight and effective techniques and processes that should be valuable to any individual and organization with a passion for learning."

—Dr. Thomas J. Malone, President, Milliken

"**C**hip Bell's book *Managers As Mentors* is one of the few things out there that recognizes the new role that managers have in building the careers of their people."

—Priscilla Claman, *Career Notes*

MANAGERS
AS
MENTORS

ALSO BY CHIP BELL

Customers As Partners

Managing Knock Your Socks Off Service
(with Ron Zemke)

Service Wisdom
(with Ron Zemke)

Understanding Training
(with Fredric Margolis)

The Trainer's Professional Development Handbook
(with Ray Bard, Leslie Stephen, and Linda Webster)

Instructing for Results
(with Fredric Margolis)

Clients and Consultants
(with Leonard Nadler)

Influencing: Marketing the Ideas That Matter

The Client-Consultant Handbook
(with Leonard Nadler)

MANAGERS AS MENTORS

Building Partnerships for Learning

CHIP R. BELL

Berrett-Koehler Publishers
San Francisco

Managers As Mentors[SM] is a service mark of Performance Research Associates, Inc.

Berrett-Koehler Publishers, Inc.
450 Sansome Street, Suite 1200
San Francisco, CA 94111-3320
Tel: (415) 288-0260   Fax: (415) 362-2512

ORDERING INFORMATION

Individual sales. Berrett-Koehler publications are available through most bookstores. They can also be ordered direct from Berrett-Koehler at the address above.
Quantity sales. Special discounts are available on quantity purchases by corporations, associations, and others. For details, contact the "Special Sales Department" at the Berrett-Koehler address above.
Orders for college textbook/course adoption use. Please contact Berrett-Koehler Publishers at the address above.
Orders by U.S. trade bookstores and wholesalers. Please contact Publishers Group West, 4065 Hollis Street, Box 8843, Emeryville, CA 94662. Tel: (510) 658-3453; 1-800-788-3123. Fax: (510) 658-1834.

Printed in the United States of America

 Printed on acid-free and recycled paper that is composed of 85% recovered fiber, including 15% post consumer waste.

Library of Congress Cataloging-in-Publication Data

Bell, Chip R.
    Managers as mentors : building partnerships for learning / Chip R.
Bell.
        p.   cm.
    Includes bibliographical references and index.
    ISBN 1-881052-92-3 (hardcover: alk. paper)
    ISBN 1-57675-034-5 (paperback: alk. paper)
    1. Mentoring in business.   2. Executives.   3. Employees–Training
of.   4. Employees–Counseling of.   I. Title.
HF5385.B45   1996
658.3'124–dc20   96-7029

First Hardcover Printing: May 1996
First Paperback Printing: January 1998

A Bard Press, Inc. Production
Austin, Texas

Executive editor: Leslie Stephen • Text/jacket design: Suzanne Pustejovsky
Copyediting: Jeff Morris • Proofreading: Deborah Costenbader • Index: Linda Webster
Composition/production: Round Rock Graphics • Cover illustration: Layne Lundström

First Paperback Printing   05 04 03 02 01 99 98   10 9 8 7 6 5 4 3
This paperback edition contains the complete text of the original hardcover edition.

DEDICATED TO

Ray U. Bell
1911–1995

CONTENTS

Prologue   *ix*

PART I

MENTORING IS...

1 The Art of Mentoring: Passing along the Wisdom   5
2 The Context for Mentoring:
    "Boss" Is a Four-Letter Word!   13
3 Leveling the Learning Field: Roles and Axioms   21
4 Mentoring in Action: A Continuing Case   29
5 Assessing Your Mentoring Talents: A Self-Check Scale   37

PART II

SURRENDERING

6 Kindling Kinship: The Power of Rapport   49
7 Avoiding Thin Ice: Advice and Feedback   57
8 Socrates' Secret Skill: Awesome Queries   67
9 Putting the "Us" in "Trust":
    Blending Humility and Confidence   77

PART III

ACCEPTING

10 Ear of an Ally: The Lost Art of Listening   87
11 "Give-and-Take" Starts with "Give":
    Distinguished Dialogues   93
12 Scared Students: When Fear and Learning Collide   103
13 Trading Power for Respect: When Pupils Are Peers   111

PART IV

GIFTING

14 The Bluebirds' Secret: The Gift of Balance   123

15 The Mentor's Greatest Gift: Passionate Connections   131

16 Mentoring on the Run: White-Water Wisdom   139

17 Mentoring Long Distance: Remote Learning   143

PART V

EXTENDING

18 The Role of Role Plays:
    Mentoring with Behavior Rehearsal   153

19 Don't Touch That Dial: Mentoring around Equipment   159

20 Managing Sweet Sorrow: Life after Mentoring   165

21 The Kaizen of Mentoring:
    Learning, Learning, Learning   169

Epilogue   175

Acknowledgments   179

Notes   181

References   183

Index   185

About the Author   190

PROLOGUE

This book started at a retirement banquet. I was a guest and the company was my client (a large company often touted in those "best run/built to last" lists). There was the usual band, banner, banter, and baked potato. There was also the customary nostalgia overload. Every aspect of the ceremony was well-trodden ground—until the final retiree was announced. For this person the applause was longer, the smiles broader, and the spirits higher.

The object of the crowd's affection was a forty-years-on-board security officer. The company president asked the security officer to come up onto the massively overdecorated stage. The audience was hushed as he listed the security officer's accomplishments. The president was followed by several senior executives, each of whom praised the security officer as mentor and friend.

The president then announced a special gift for this mentor of mentors. Everyone waited in suspense. What special present could appropriately celebrate the contribution this man had made to so many?

The first clue was the stir and side conversations emerging from the back of the room as a man appeared in the doorway. I could hardly believe my eyes! Down the long aisle from the back door to the podium walked one of the most famous people in the business world. His face was familiar to everyone in the room—and, for that matter, almost everyone in the country.

The surprise visitor walked straight to the security officer and embraced him warmly. With tears welling up in his eyes, he thanked the retiree for being a wonderful tutor during his brief two-year stint with the company early in his career. He then left the banquet hall to board his limo and fly in his private jet back to the opposite coast. The crowd sat stunned, no one speaking for a long time. Then, one by one, they filed to the front to express their gratitude to all the retirees.

I will never forget the power of that evening. It started me thinking about the gift of mentoring. What exactly did the security officer do to evoke such devotion? What contribution did he make to gain such universal admiration? The evening made me remember the many mentors who have blessed my life. What gift could I offer in return?

This book is my gift. Thank you—Ray, Avis, Mrs. Pope, Dr. Saye, Sergeant Duckett, Captain Jack, Chuck, Luther, Tony, Bruce, Fredric, Len, Malcolm, Gordon, Geoff, Larry, Richard, Ron, Tom, Kristin, Kathy, Glenn, Grady, Jimmie, Karen, Steve, Ken, Oren, Nancy, and all the other many mentors of my life.

WHAT THIS BOOK IS ABOUT

The mentor is a teacher, a guide, a sage, and foremost a person acting to the best of his or her ability in a whole and compassionate way in plain view of the protégé. No greater helping or healing can occur than that induced by a model of compassion and authenticity. Mentoring is about being real, being a catalyst, and sometimes being a kind of prophet. It is therefore far more art than science. It is about personal power, not expert or role power. The most powerful and most difficult part of mentoring is being who you are.

This is not to imply that a mentor must be some kind of superhero without flaws, doubts, or mistakes. Fundamentally, mentoring is about growing—mentors growing protégés, protégés growing with mentors. The core of a mentoring relationship is more about a mutual search than about wisdom passage. As a collective pursuit, mentoring works best when mentors are focused on building, not boasting.

The anthropologist Carlos Castaneda used the word "magic" to describe his unique mentoring relationship with the Yaqui medicine man, Don Juan—and truly there is a magical quality about the spirit of the mentoring process when it takes on a life of its own and leads mentor and protégé through an experience of shared discovery. The challenge of helping another see things in a new way has had many labels down through the centuries. Biblical writers used fishing analogies and told of removing scales from eyes. The philosopher Ram Dass referred to it as "a dance."

However, mentoring magic cannot be a solo performance. It is not a one-way, master-to-novice transaction. To be effective and lasting, it must be accomplished through a two-way relationship—the synchronized efforts of two people. The synchrony and synergy of mentoring are what give it a dance-like quality. They are also what make it magical.

This is not the first book on mentoring—nor the last. But from what I have seen, it is the only one to date that is grounded in a true partnership philosophy. My take on mentoring with a partnership philosophy is this: Assume that all your future employees will be independently wealthy, headstrong, purpose-seeking volunteers who love to acquire learning but hate to surrender liberty. If you are now thrust into an active, leadership role in a real-life learning play, how will you approach your fellow actors?

This book is also about power-free facilitation of learning. It is about teaching through consultation and affection rather than constriction and assessment. It views learning as an expansive, unfolding process rather than an evaluative, narrowing effort. It is the instruction book on how to do synchronized magic.

This is not a philosophy book, although it is grounded in a very specific conviction. This is a workbook, filled with ideas, suggestions, how-tos, and resources. If this copy ends up dog-eared, underlined, and passed around, it will mean that I have succeeded in making it a practical book—perhaps even a fun book as well as a soul-searching one. It is intended to be a tool for one component of the leader's responsibility—helping another learn and grow.

WHY THIS BOOK IS IMPORTANT TODAY

We enter a peculiar era in the world of enterprise. Revolutionary change renders skills and knowledge obsolete almost overnight. Peter Vaill's term "permanent white water" has been used to characterize the feel of the workplace today. Likewise, success comes through creative adaptation and innovative breakthroughs rather than replicating the tried (tired) and true (not new). "If it ain't broke, don't fix it" has been replaced by "If it ain't broke, break it." Almost overnight, employees can go from champ to chump unless they stay perpetually honed and forever in a ready position. High-level knowledge requirements are moving to low levels in the organization, meaning smartness can no longer be the badge only of bosses.

All of this implies a requirement for a *learning organization*. This term, made famous by Peter Senge in his best-selling book *The Fifth Discipline,* denotes an enterprise that has growth, learning, improvement, and everlasting experimentation woven into the fabric of its culture. "The ability to learn faster than your competition," said consultant Arie De Geus, formerly of Royal Dutch/Shell, "may be your only sustainable competitive advantage."

Learning organizations value creativity over control. They buck the tenets of old-style corporations by fostering an environment of risk taking. Tom Peters and Bob Waterman, in their 1982 bestseller *In Search of Excellence,* take the same perspective by telling stories of corporate skunkworks—those underground, internal entrepreneurs who pursue innovation typically at odds with the organizational bureaucracy, which values order and procedure above all else.

There is another factor of business life, now undergoing a metamorphosis, that fuels the rationale for this book: the relationship between boss and subordinate. The old model of leader as authority and corporate parent has been and is being altered to one of leader as supporter, enabler, even partner. As workers increasingly demonstrate that they have the maturity and competence to operate effectively with limited supervision, empowerment has become a necessity rather than a fad. Leaders unable to let go of the reins of power are fast being replaced by leaders who view their relationship with associates as being that of liberator, barrier remover, facilitator, and mentor.

The requirement for constant learning and the modification of the leader's role call for a new kind of manager. This book has been crafted to provide supervisors and managers both the competence and the confidence to address these two factors. While managers frequently perform their bossing in a group context, as with a team, the lion's share of the manager's time is spent one-on-one. Therefore, this book largely focuses on the interpersonal encounters of leaders. Mentoring is predominantly a one-person-at-a-time activity.

The definition of leader could be expanded to include anyone in a role (short or long term) whose primary goal is to influence another to important efforts or outcome. Given the flattening of organizations, more often than not the mentoring a person receives may come from a peer. For this reason, I have included a chapter on peer mentoring.

HOW TO GET THE MOST FROM THIS BOOK

Most books are written to be read from front to back. This book is not one of them. However, you will benefit from reading the first section first (chapters 1 through 5). Chapter 5 contains a self-scoring instrument referenced in several chapters throughout the book. To derive the greatest learning from those later chapters, complete and score this instrument before proceeding beyond chapter 5.

Before reading any chapter, start with a goal. Select a relationship you seek to improve, a skill you want to enhance, or a mentoring problem you want to solve. Choose the chapter that seems best suited to addressing that relationship, skill, or challenge. As you read the chapter, make notes on how you might apply the techniques found in the chapter. To help you zero in on the best chapter for your need, below is a brief description of the objective of each chapter.

Chapter 1: The Art of Mentoring: Passing along the Wisdom. This opening chapter outlines what mentoring is (and is not), mentoring traps to avoid, and perspectives about how to make the mentoring relationship effective. This chapter also provides an overview of the mentoring structure used to organize the book.

Chapter 2: The Context for Mentoring: "Boss" Is a Four-Letter Word. This chapter seeks to outline where mentoring fits into the rapidly changing role of the person charged with supervisory or leadership responsibilities as organizations flatten, the span of control widens, and the traditional role of boss changes. This chapter positions mentoring as one of the most important roles of the manager or supervisor of the future.

Chapter 3: Leveling the Learning Field: Roles and Axioms offers the underlying philosophy of the mentor-protégé partnership. This chapter is designed to set the tone and communicate the attitude and belief system woven throughout the book.

Chapter 4: Mentoring in Action: A Continuing Case has a simple and singular purpose: to present the feel and drama of mentoring. Often participants in coaching and mentoring classes ask: Could you show a movie of what solid mentoring looks like, so we could know it when we see it? There may be one, but I have yet to see it. However, this chapter attempts to provide the "screenplay" for such a movie.

Chapter 5: Assessing Your Mentoring Talents: A Self-Check Scale. This is the chapter with the self-scoring instrument. Since several chapters have sidebars that apply the results of this instrument, you should read this chapter before reading others. Read chapters 1 through 5 first, then select whatever chapter fits your need.

Chapter 6: Kindling Kinship: The Power of Rapport makes the point that the way the mentoring relationship begins strongly influences how effective it is later. This chapter provides both perspectives and techniques for getting the mentoring relationship off to a solid start.

Chapter 7: Avoiding Thin Ice: Advice and Feedback. Most people think the main thing mentors do is give advice—but if done inappropriately, advice giving is one of the most dangerous actions a mentor can take. The first part of this chapter provides techniques for giving advice while minimizing resistance; the second part examines ways giving feedback differs from giving advice and how you can make your comments count.

Chapter 8: Socrates' Secret Skill: Awesome Queries focuses on the power of asking questions to gain protégé acceptance. Everyone knows how to ask questions, but good mentoring uses inquiry as a tool to enrich the relationship while facilitating insight and discovery. Mastering the techniques in this chapter can benefit all interpersonal relationships.

Chapter 9: Putting the "Us" in "Trust": Blending Humility with Confidence focuses on ways to narrow the emotional distance between mentor and protégé. This chapter outlines power-reducing techniques to create a level playing field for a productive mentoring relationship.

Chapter 10: Ear of an Ally: The Lost Art of Listening focuses on the importance and power of acceptance through listening. The initial temptation may be to skip this chapter thinking, "I know how to listen!" Some readers have indicated that this may be the most powerful chapter in the book because it offers a much deeper and richer definition of listening than that generally discussed in how-to books.

Chapter 11: "Give-and-Take" Starts with "Give": Distinguished Dialogues is not a chapter about questions and answers; it is a chapter that offers interpersonal tools on how to make a discussion more of an insightful conversation. This chapter takes Socrates' secret (chapter 8) to an advanced level of application, complete with techniques for restarting a stalled or sidetracked discussion or stopping a discussion that has become unproductive.

Chapter 12: Scared Students: When Fear and Learning Collide. One of the greatest barriers to learning is fear. Most leader-follower relationships have some element of anxiety, given the ever-present existence of position power. Likewise, most organizations still spend a lot of energy on evaluation, testing, and judging—all potential anxiety producers. This chapter examines ways to make a mentoring relationship a safe haven from apprehension for the protégé, thus a healthy environment for learning.

Chapter 13: Trading Power for Respect: When Pupils Are Peers. Most of this book is concerned with mentoring people who are subordinate in the organizational hierarchy. However, chapter 13 focuses on mentoring colleagues or peers, in which the principal issue is resistance, and addresses ways to creatively handle a variety of interpersonal challenges of peer mentoring.

Chapter 14: The Bluebirds' Secret: The Gift of Balance explores the role of balance in fostering growth. One of a mentor's most challenging dilemmas is to find a balance between giving the protégé freedom and providing guidance. The "when to hold 'em, when to fold 'em" challenge is especially tricky when the protégé approaches mastery and independence.

Chapter 15: The Mentor's Greatest Gift: Passionate Connections addresses the power of passion, spirit, and enthusiasm in the mentoring relationship. Countless studies show that the quality and quantity of learning are dramatically enhanced by the learner's excitement for learning. The mentor can play a crucial role in fostering this passion by displaying a sincere enthusiasm for the process.

Chapter 16: Mentoring on the Run: White-Water Wisdom. The formidable task most mentors have in today's "Time's up!" work world is giving the protégé attention when other priorities invade the calendar. Yet quality attention, even if brief, can enhance the relationship by communicating caring and concern. The chapter provides practical ways to mentor effectively when time is limited.

Chapter 17: Mentoring Long Distance: Remote Learning addresses another challenge many mentors face: how to effectively mentor associates in other places or those with whom they have only intermittent contact. Just because the mentor is not present does not mean there is no way to be generous with learning facilitation. This chapter offers an array of ideas and approaches.

Chapter 18: The Role of Role Plays: Mentoring with Behavior Rehearsal discusses ways to extend learning by adding a powerful learning technique to the mentoring relationship. When the goal of the mentoring process is acquiring an interpersonal competence, role plays ("behavior rehearsal") can be a boon to effective performance. This chapter challenges much of the conventional wisdom on role plays.

Chapter 19: Don't Touch That Dial: Mentoring around Equipment. Sometimes the mentor and protégé are involved in learning to use equipment. Psychomotor skill building carries special challenges addressed by this chapter. Numerous techniques are provided for helping protégés learn to use tools and equipment.

Chapter 20: Managing Sweet Sorrow: Life after Mentoring. Almost every mentoring relationship eventually comes to an end. The protégé outgrows the wisdom of the mentor; the protégé's learning needs shift to an area requiring a different mentor; the protégé or the mentor moves to a new role or place. How the relationship ends affects the readiness of both to establish new mentoring relationships, so the parting is a potent platform for continuing growth.

Chapter 21: The Kaizen of Mentoring: Learning, Learning, Learning provides perspectives and resources for the mentor's continuing learning.

Since effective mentors are more fellow learners than teachers, perpetual growth must be modeled and managed. This chapter shows how.

Share this book with your colleagues and associates; it has no secrets aimed at making you look good to an unknowing subordinate. The book is grounded in a partnership philosophy. The more you know about how to mentor, the better the mentoring relationship will work for you. The same is true for the protégé. Some have found discussing the book helpful in improving the process of mentoring. Do what works for you.

The words I use for the players in the mentoring partnership are chosen more for convenience than for any other reason. "Mentors" are leaders who engage in deliberate actions aimed at promoting learning; "leader," "manager," or "coach" would serve as well. Likewise, "protégé" refers to the primary beneficiary of the mentoring effort; "associate," "subordinate," "colleague," "partner," or "follower" could have been used. As long as we are clear on which person we mean, the labels can be changed to fit individual preferences and situations.

You may notice that two leadership challenges are missing from this book—the poor performer, and the mentoring of protégés with special mentoring needs (that is, diversity situations). The singular focus of this book is on influencing *learning* that impacts performance, not on other factors impacting performance. Mentoring is the one component of the coaching role that deals with addition—the need to *add* a skill, competence, or understanding. When the goal is correction—the need to *fix* a performance problem or discrepancy—it is coaching territory outside the bounds of a purely mentoring role.

Mentoring is often used as an affirmative action tool for remedying disparities in opportunities for the disadvantaged or for groups such as ethnic minorities who are underrepresented in some strata of the organization. The underutilization of any talent, regardless of gender, race, nationality, creed, physical or mental challenge, or life choice, adversely affects the long-term success of an organization. Consequently, special mentoring programs can be a benefit to better talent use and more equitable opportunity. However, the actual practice of effective mentoring (the skills, philosophy, and techniques) should be essentially the same for all mentors and all protégés. And this book is about mentoring, not mentoring programs.

The cover of this book symbolizes both the mentoring process and the mentoring outcome. The process is an unfolding, changing effort, like trees growing tall and healthy. The color green was chosen for its many connotations. Green has always characterized growth (the color of spring) and newness. Green traffic lights imply progress—they say "Go!"

Green can also connote prosperity. I hope you prosper from and enjoy this book. I would very much like your feedback on its usefulness, as well as your ideas on ways it might be improved in future editions. You will find my address at the bottom of the last page. Drop me a line, fax, or e-mail note, or give me a call. Happy mentoring!

Chip R. Bell
Dallas, Texas
February 1996

PART

I

MENTORING IS...

Take a minute to recall the people in your life who were effective at helping you learn something important. (I'll wait.) *My grandfather taught me a lot about fishing; Ms. Ethridge gave me piano lessons; Len Nadler helped me learn about human resource development; and Bilijack, my son, showed me some awesome soccer plays. Over the course of our lives, learning comes from many people, in many places, and through many events.*

What are the reasons that people sometimes learn and sometimes fail to learn? What are the reasons that some people are skilled at helping others with personal or professional growth and some are not? Why does mentoring sometimes make an impact and at other times seem a complete waste of time and energy? What conditions and competencies spark discovery, insight, and understanding?

The complete answers to questions like these could occupy volumes—and you're holding only a single book. As you will see, there are *tools, tips, tactics, and techniques that make mentoring easier to understand, more effective, and a lot more fun—but to become good at the game, we must first mark off the playing field. Before we learn the pointers, we need to be clear on the meaning of mentoring and in harmony with the conditions conducive to its effectiveness.*

The goal of the next five chapters is to explain the arena or context of mentoring. Mentoring will be defined as "the act of helping another learn." Mentoring is traditionally thought of as a transaction between a tutor and somebody else's subordinate. However, Managers As Mentors *will focus largely on the leader mentoring a follower. This will require a unique alteration in the relationship—actions aimed at eliminating (or at least reducing) the role that position power plays in the tutelage.*

The mentoring arena is filled with assumptions about the way people learn, roles mentors can play, qualities mentors should pursue, and traps mentors need to avoid. Since the mentor is also a learner, the intent of the next few chapters is to prompt self-examination, to advocate clarity of mission, and to nurture the linkage of who we are with what we do.

1

THE ART OF MENTORING

Passing along the Wisdom

ENTOR: the word conjures up an image of a seasoned corporate sage conversing with a naive, wet-behind-the-ears young recruit. The conversation would probably be laced with informal rules, closely guarded secrets, and "I remember back in '57 . . ." stories of daredevil heroics and too-close-to-call tactics. Mentoring has an almost heady, academic sound, reserved solely for workers

in white collars whose fathers advised, "Get to know ol' Charlie."

More recently the term "mentor" became connected less with privilege and more with affirmative action. Minority employees got assigned a mentor to expedite their route through glass ceilings, beyond old-boy networks and the private winks formerly reserved for WASP males. Such mentors sometimes salved the consciences of those who bravely talked goodness but became squeamish if expected to spearhead courageous acts. These mentoring programs sounded contemporary and forward-thinking. Some were of great service, but many were just lip service.

But what is mentoring, really? When the package is unwrapped and the politically correct is scraped away, what's left? A mentor is defined in the dictionary as "a wise, trusted advisor . . . a teacher or coach." Such a simple definition communicates its plain-vanilla context. A mentor is simply someone who helps someone else learn something the learner would otherwise have learned less well, more slowly, or not at all. Notice the power-free nature of this definition; mentors are not power figures.

> **❝Learning is not attained by chance, it must be sought for with ardor and attended to with diligence.❞**
>
> — Abigail Adams, 1780

The traditional use of the word "mentor" denotes a person outside one's usual chain of command—from the junior's point of view, someone who "helps me understand the informal system and offers guidance on how to be successful in this crazy organization." Not all mentors are supervisors, but all effective supervisors should be mentors. Mentoring is typically focused on one person; group mentoring is training or teaching, subjects that are beyond the scope of this book.

Good leaders do a lot of things. Good leaders communicate a clear vision and articulate a precise direction. Good leaders provide performance feedback, inspire and encourage, and, when necessary, discipline. Good leaders also mentor. Mentoring is the part of a leader's role that has growth as its outcome.

THE FIRST MENTOR

The word "mentor" comes from *The Odyssey,* written by the Greek poet Homer. As Odysseus ("Ulysses," in the Latin translation) is preparing to go fight the Trojan War, he realizes he is leaving behind his one and only heir, Telemachus. Since "Telie" (as he was known to his buddies) is only in junior high, and since wars tend to drag on for years (the Trojan War lasted ten), Odysseus recognizes that Telie needs to be coached on how to "king" while Daddy is off fighting. He hires a trusted family friend named Mentor to be Telie's tutor. Mentor is both wise and sensitive—two important ingredients of world-class mentoring.

The history of the word "mentor" is instructive for several reasons. First, it underscores the legacy nature of mentoring. Like Odysseus, great leaders strive to leave behind a benefaction of added value. Second, Mentor (the old man) combined the wisdom of experience with the sensitivity of a fawn in his attempts to convey kingship skills to young Telemachus. We all know the challenge of conveying our hard-won wisdom to another without resistance. The successful mentor is able to circumvent resistance.

Homer characterizes Mentor as a family friend. The symbolism contained in this phrase is apropos to contemporary mentors. Effective mentors are like friends in that their goal is to create a safe context for growth. They are also like family in that their focus is to offer an unconditional, faithful acceptance of the protégé. Friends work to add and multiply, not subtract. Family members care, even in the face of mistakes and errors.

Superior mentors know how adults learn. Operating out of their intuition or on what they have learned from books, classes, or other mentors, the best mentors recognize that they

Effective mentors are like friends in that their goal is to create a safe context for growth.

are, first and foremost, facilitators and catalysts in a process of discovery and insight. They know that mentoring is not about smart comments, eloquent lectures, or clever quips. Mentors practice their skills with a combination of never-ending compassion, crystal-clear communication, and a sincere joy in the role of being a helper along a journey toward mastery.

Just like the first practitioner of their craft, mentors love learning, not teaching. They treasure sharing rather than showing off, giving rather than boasting. Great mentors are not only devoted fans of their protégés, they are loyal fans of the dream of what the protégé can become with their guidance.

TRAPS TO AVOID

There are countless traps along the path of mentordom. Mentoring can be a power trip for those seeking an admirer, a manifestation of greed for those who must have slaves. Mentoring can be a platform for proselytizing a cause or crusade, a strong tale told to an innocent or unknowing listener. However, the traps of power, greed, and crusading all pale when compared with the more subtle "watch out fors" listed below. Review the list; keep the traps in mind throughout the book; search for them within yourself. By the time you've read the last page, you will perhaps have learned to avoid those to which you are most susceptible.

I can help

When is help helpful, and when is it harmful? People inclined to be charitable with their time, energy, and expertise often try to help when what the learner actually needs is to struggle and find her own way. Here's a test: If you ask the protégé, "Can I help?" and she says no, how do you feel? Be honest with yourself. If you react with even a trace of rejection and self-pity, this may be your trap to avoid.

Charles J. ("Chuck") Cooley was an early mentor in my career. I had just assumed supervision of the training department of what was then North Carolina National Bank (now NationsBank), reporting to Chuck, then personnel director. I needed to hire a new assistant training director. Chuck offered suggestions and advice about ways to recruit a winner. My favorite candidate was a young man with a very impressive résumé. However, his graduate degree from an Ivy League school had clouded my objectivity, and I overlooked flaws in his interpersonal style.

Chuck, formerly a crackerjack recruiter with a major manufacturing company, could have intervened and kept me from hiring a person he knew would ultimately not perform at the bank's performance standards. His allowing me to make this selection mistake was a major gift in my professional development. The young man, whom I ultimately terminated, also benefited—he pursued a career track at another organization more suited to his style.

I know best

Some people become mentors because they enjoy being recognized as someone in the know. They relish the affirmations from protégés who brag to others about their helpful mentor. They especially like protégés who regularly compliment them on their contribution.

This is a trap! You may get off track and end up using the protégé for your own recognition needs. The test? If your protégé comes to you and says that he has found someone else who might be more helpful as a mentor, how do you react? If you feel more than mild and momentary disappointment, beware! This may be your special trap.

I can help you get ahead

Mentors can be useful in getting around organizational barriers, getting into offices otherwise closed, and getting special tips useful in climbing the ladder of success. As sometime king makers, their promises carry an "I can get it for you wholesale" seduction.

All these "gettings" can be valuable and important. They can also add a bartering, sinister component to an otherwise promising relationship. The "you scratch my back, and . . ." approach to mentoring relationships can infuse a score-keeping dimension that is detrimental to both parties. While reciprocity can be important, a tit-for-tat aspect can lead one person in the relationship to a score-keeping, "You owe me one" view of the relationship.

You need me

When mentors feel that their protégés need them, they are laying the groundwork for a relationship based on dependence. While many mentor-protégé partnerships begin with some degree of dependence, the goal is to transform the relationship into one of strength and interdependence. A relationship based on dependence can ultimately become a source of resentment for the protégé, false power for the mentor.

In my early days as a consultant, I had a colleague who was very important in helping me learn what he called "the stuff the textbooks don't tell you." He was about fifteen years my senior in age and probably twenty-five years in experience. "Consulting is an apprentice model," he would say, and he was clearly a master craftsman and teacher. However, as I gained experience, his "lessons" took on a sometimes critical and often smothering tone. I became less enthusiastic about our talks; he grew more demanding of my loyalty. Fault lay on both sides. Sadly, as the mentoring relationship came to an end, so did our friendship.

If the protégé views the mentoring process as a chore or a necessary ritual, it is generally a dependent relationship that will not be allowed to grow up. Remember, the focus should be on helping the protégé become strong, not on helping the protégé feel better about being weak.

The focus should be on helping the protégé become strong, not on helping the protégé feel better about being weak.

There are other traps, but these are the ones that most frequently raise their ugly heads to sabotage healthy relationships. Great mentors are not immune to traps; great mentors recognize traps and work to compensate for them. What follows will be ideas and instruction useful in minimizing the impact of these traps.

SAGE: THE RECIPE FOR MENTORING

There are many ways to bake a cake; the same is true for mentoring. The mentoring recipe found in this book will be built around the belief that great mentoring requires four core competencies, each of which can be applied in many ways. All four have been selected for their effective blend with power-free learning facilitation. Not accidentally, the first letters of these four recipe ingredients spell the word "SAGE"—a helpful mnemonic as well as a symbolic representation of the goal, the transfer of wisdom. Mentoring greats are effective at

Surrendering, **A**ccepting, **G**ifting, and **E**xtending.

Most leaders are socially conditioned to *drive* the process of learning; great mentors *surrender* to it. Driving the process has many unfortunate effects. It tends to cause resistance; it minimizes the potential for serendipitous growth, and it tilts the focus from competence to control.

If there is one word many leaders hate, it is the word "surrender." However, by *surrendering* I don't mean losing, but yielding to a flow greater than either player in the process. The dictionary defines "surrender" as "to yield possession of." Mentors who attempt to hold, own, or control the process deprive it of the freedom needed to foster discovery.

Accepting is the act of inclusion. Acceptance is what the late psychologist Carl Rogers labeled "unconditional positive regard." Most leaders are taught to focus on exclusion. Exclusion is associated with preferential treatment, and with presumption, arrogance, and insolence—growth killers all. The verb "accept," however, implies ridding oneself of bias, preconceived judgments, and human labeling. Accepting is embracing, rather than evaluating or judging.

Gifting is the act of generosity. Gifting, as opposed to giving, means bestowing something of value upon another without expecting anything in return. Mentors have many gifts to share. When they bestow those gifts abundantly and unconditionally, they strengthen the relationship and keep it healthy. Gifting is the antithesis of taking or using manipulatively. It is at the opposite end of the spectrum from greed.

Extending means pushing the relationship beyond its expected boundaries. Mentors who extend are willing to give up the relationship in the interest of growth, to seek alternative ways to foster growth. They recognize that the protégé's learning can occur and be enhanced in many and mysterious ways.

The gifts of mentoring—advice, feedback, support, passion, balance—are truly *the* main event. Most mentors begin there and get resistance. *Surrendering* and *Accepting* are crucial preambles, for they help "level the learning field" and ensure that *Gifting* has the power and impact intended. *Extending* helps minimize the protégé's dependence on the mentor.

Except for love, there is no greater gift one can give another than the gift of growth.

These four core competencies (capabilities or proficiencies) will serve as the organizing structure for the rest of this book. Their sequence is important. The process of mentoring begins with surrendering and ends with extending. Under each of the four competencies you will find several chapters full of techniques for demonstrating that competence effectively. Before we get into a discussion of techniques, we'll use the next few chapters to explore the mentoring arena—the role and responsibility of the mentor. The final chapter will be crafted around your continued growth as a mentor.

Mentoring is an honor. Except for love, there is no greater gift one can give another than the gift of growth. It is a rare privilege to help another learn, have the relevant wisdom useful to another, and have someone who can benefit from that wisdom. This book is crafted with a single goal: to help you exercise that honor and privilege in a manner that benefits you and all those you influence.

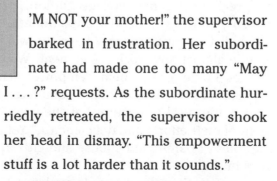

THE CONTEXT FOR MENTORING

"Boss" Is a Four-Letter Word!

I 'M NOT your mother!" the supervisor barked in frustration. Her subordinate had made one too many "May I . . . ?" requests. As the subordinate hurriedly retreated, the supervisor shook her head in dismay. "This empowerment stuff is a lot harder than it sounds."

The evolution of bossing—of what it means to be in charge—is a challenge for many supervisors and managers whose bossing lessons came from stern teachers, tight-lipped drill sergeants, and autocratic coaches. All know the old way is unpopular; most know it is also ineffective. The be-a-buddy approach seems to erode respect in times of conflict. The benevolent-parent approach seems to get compliance (through guilt or fear), but little commitment. And the plain-vanilla coordinator/administrator seems to foster a lot of efficiency but little enthusiasm.

> **"In times of massive change, learners inherit the world, while the learned remain beautifully equipped to deal with a world that no longer exists."**
>
> — Eric Hoffer

What does bossing need to be like in this era of the knowledge worker, where subordinates act more like independent agents than willing servants? And if empowerment is the goal, what happens to important virtues like control, consistency, and equity? As one crusty manager asked, "What do I now kick and take if not butts and names?"

The boss of yesteryear held the reins tight lest employees get lazy and fail to work. We now are learning that today's subordinates are far more likely to act as adults when treated as adults. Employees who manage tight family budgets, buy and sell real estate, pay college tuition, prepare complex tax returns, and juggle dentist appointments with soccer games and ballet lessons probably have the wisdom and maturity to handle almost any work assignment. We can surmise that no one at home gives them "empowerment" or "appropriate supervision." No one at home completes their annual performance appraisal to ensure that they get "an accurate assessment of their efforts and deficiencies." Yet they usually manage the roles of parent and spouse and citizen just fine, thank you very much!

Just as the role of boss is evolving, the rules of the game are changing with it. Yesterday's ratio of five subordinates reporting to every supervisor is more like forty to one today. Employees want to be left alone or to work with their peers;

they resent *super*vision. The proliferation of self-directed work teams suggests "No bosses allowed." Is it any wonder that organizational turnover and elimination of positions has happened mostly in that space above the front line of the organizational chart and below the executive suite? Middle managers are scrambling to figure out the new rules of bossing. They are becoming alienated, frustrated—and downright scared.

The lament of many of today's supervisors and managers goes something like this: "I worked hard to get into a position where I could give orders instead of taking orders. Now, either the position is being eliminated or they tell me giving orders is obsolete! What am I supposed to do? How can I find some contribution that is valued enough to bring me a little job security? What does supervision mean today?"

The new leader's role is that of partner—one who supports employees. "Partner" does not mean "servant." The word "servant" (with a hat tip to Robert Greenleaf!) implies deference; "partner" implies mutuality. "Servant" calls for power over; "partner" requires power with. Servant connotes compliance; partner connotes community. Servants acquiesce; partners assert. Servants show patronage; partners show passion.

While the concept of turning the organization upside down makes great material for motivational speeches, it suggests that if the old pyramid was wrong (head dude at the top; worker bees at the bottom, serving customers), the thing to do is flip the chart. Since audiences were rarely at the top, the idea of seeing the top underneath was rather appealing: "It's about time we got the Old Man where he belongs." But pyramids, whether right side up or upside down, are all about hierarchy and power; partnerships are about power-free relationships. The organization of the future will be more like a circle, with the customers in the middle and all employees working in partnership to serve them.

Competitive advantage today requires cutting-edge innovation, distinctive service, and lightning-fast responsiveness. That advantage calls for a work force highly committed to success and passionate about quality. Up against these challenges,

Just as the role of boss is evolving, the rules of the game are changing with it.

organizations are asking employees to do more with less—without the ability to promise, as in the past, "In exchange for your commitment we will take care of you until you die." How can an organization get passion without promise? Devotion without dividends? The secret may lie in creating an environment in which leaders treat followers more like partners than underlings.

The new "partner-leader" focuses less on sovereignty and more on support. Controlling takes a back seat to coaching. Position-based power—the "Because I said so!" type—has become the last resort of the inept. But what do leaders do as partners? How do they fulfill their "in charge" responsibilities when power is no longer the medium of exchange?

Below are five keys to effective partnership. Consider them as a part of the mantle of leadership and examine their impact.

PUSH EMPLOYEES TO TAKE RISKS

When managers discuss empowerment, they lament that employees have far more power and authority than they use—and this is generally true. But if you bring together a group of employees, they will gripe about their lack of authority. Why this paradox? Because empowerment (or lack of it) is often coded communication for fear of failure. Many of us have pent-up childhood memories of what happened when "exacting parent" was mixed with "error-prone child." The residue plays out in adult days as a timidity about making mistakes. For many people, erasing concern over authority-figure disapproval can take a lifetime.

True partners view mistakes as opportunities to learn, grow, and solve problems. Leader-partners encourage their employees to take it to the limit and push the edge of the envelope—which means occasionally overshooting the mark. "Failing on purpose" means failing consistent with or in sync with the mission or vision. For example, if your mission is

Leader-partners encourage their employees to take it to the limit and push the edge of the envelope—which means occasionally overshooting the mark.

about high quality, "failing on purpose" might mean going overboard with quality. A "go the extra mile for the customer" unit vision or purpose might have an employee going an extra mile—and a half! The goal is not to promote errors per se or to set employees up to get hurt, but rather to encourage employees to experience the limits and, if they go too far, learn that the leader's response will be support and coaching rather than punishment and rebuke. How would Thomas Edison or Marie Curie have fared under a supervisor?

BE KNOWN AS A DRAMATIC LISTENER

Many leaders brag about how well they listen to employees. However, those pursuing partnership with employees listen in a manner that makes subordinates understand that their input is valued and makes a difference. Emphasis shifts from the leader's actions to the subordinate's experience. Partner-leaders listen, listen, listen—and then respond, respond, respond. Does this mean you always have to do what they say? No. Employees don't want their leaders to consent, they want them to confirm.

Consider this: If you were on trial for being a poor listener, would your subordinates have enough evidence to get you either convicted or acquitted? Great leaders pursue the up-front, face-to-face, clean communication that fosters truth, not sterilized diplomacy. Partner-leaders know that partnerships falter, not because the people in them fail to *speak* the truth, but because they fail to *assert* the truth. And assertion starts with the leader.

BE A MODEL OF YOUR VALUES

When I was a teenager heading out of the house for a Saturday evening of freedom and fun, my dad would advise me, "Son, don't forget who you are!" My rebellious internal retort

*Leaders foster part-
nership by making
sure their mouths
match their moves.*

generally had a smart-aleck tone. Yet I have more than once repeated the familiar line to *my* son. One weekend, home from college, he was heading out for the evening. "Don't forget who you are!" I ritualistically cautioned, just as my dad had done. He stopped at the front door, turned, and said, "Dad, I know what it means to be a Bell!" For the first time, I realized fully what my father had been communicating. Family, team, unit, department, or division all imply a group of people united by a shared vision, collective values, and a common picture of "I know what it means to be an Acme engineer!"

But clarity and confidence in a mission or vision are not assured by clever words on a page or banner. Leaders foster partnership by making sure their mouths match their moves. Announcing one message and acting another fosters cynicism, disrupts unity, and breeds distrust and dissonance. Partnership flourishes through never-ending congruence and ceaseless consistency. When creeds are at odds with deeds, doubts begin to surface and the spirit of involvement fades from commitment and contribution to self-serving efforts or begrudging compliance.

CELEBRATE, CELEBRATE, CELEBRATE

Great partners never take their partners for granted. As my Uncle Boyd said of his fifty-plus-year marriage to Martha Jane: "We got married, but we never quit courting." Wise leaders look for ways to tell customers, other leaders, and vendors, the "You're not going to believe this!" stories about employees— especially in the employee's presence. People like affirmation; people need affirmation; people grow with affirmation. Great relationships start with an affirming attitude and end with an affirming expression. Show employees that you're their biggest fan.

Leader-partners look for ways to celebrate that let employees know clearly *why* they are being affirmed. My wife and I stopped in a small restaurant for breakfast. Our waiter had on a name tag and an "Employee of the Month" pin. "Congratulations!" I told him. "I see you're the Employee of the Month. What did you do to get such a distinction?" He paused and responded in a flat monotone, "I guess it was my turn." It is central when employees are celebrated that they are clear on what inspired the affirmation. Celebrations begin with "see"!

SERVE AS MENTOR

Perhaps the most contributive role of today's leader is that of mentor. Effective leaders care about the competence of their associates. Successful leaders abhor skill obsolescence and out-of-date tools and methods. They are always on the lookout for ways to help associates grow. As mentors, they are also learners; they learn with others and from others.

Mentors are the model employees in the learning organizations of the future. As organizations encounter greater and greater challenges from competitors skilled in stealth, speed, and scrappiness, their success hangs on their adaptability and resourcefulness. These traits are effectively practiced only in organizations that reward experimentation, support learning, and eliminate barriers to imagination. Learning organizations will be the surviving enterprises of tomorrow, and the leaders who remain in these organizations will be those most adept at helping others learn. Partners who learn together earn together.

Partners who learn together earn together.

This book is about mentoring—but at a deeper level it is about successful partnering. There is an expression in golf: "playing over your head." It means that a golfer is playing at an unexplained level of excellence in which serendipity and the extraordinary seem the momentary norm. Effective leadership is a relationship of leaders and followers who seek to honor their partnership by "learning over their heads." Such leadership is practiced in its purest form in a mentoring relationship.

LEVELING THE LEARNING FIELD

3

Roles and Axioms

EVERY PROFESSION gets sidetracked from time to time. Physicians think about pills and paperwork and neglect patients. Preachers puzzle over the proper gospel and forget about souls. Sellers think about sales and ignore customers. And mentors think about topics and smart delivery instead of their protégés.

Wise mentors, however, remember their responsibility to partner with their protégés. Mentoring should begin as a partnership between a mentor and protégé for the purpose of mutual growth. The quality of this relationship dramatically affects how much the protégé and the mentor grow.

ROLES MENTORS PLAY

The roles mentors assume can either enhance or impede the learning process. Below are a few of the roles mentors play when mentoring. The mottoes reveal implied assumptions and may help you become more aware of the hidden whys behind any role or combination of roles you have adopted.

The wizard

"Listen to my counsel, heed my word, and you may succeed, grasshopper!"

The wizard style has a guru quality; the focus is on the genius of the guru. The goal of learning is the wizard's approval, not the protégé's subsequent performance. To the protégé, the wizard style can seem pompous, egotistical, and mentor-centered. There is probably a bit of this approach in all of us, given the right opportunity.

One of my early mentors was a brilliant organizational psychologist. His manner was always all-knowing, and his advice typically contained a patronizing "You're not really smart enough to understand this" tone. For a long time I felt I would always be inadequate and rather ignorant in his eyes. I had to wade through my own doubts and insecurities to finally reach a point where his judgments ceased to concern me. I often think of how much more I could have learned from him had he used a more accepting, less critical approach.

The comic

"Keep 'em laughing and they'll go away feeling good."

The comic confuses entertainment with learning. Effective mentors know that levity and joy are important ingredients in learning. However, mentors with mostly comic skills can inadvertently shift the focus from acquiring competence to having a good time.

One mentor I found particularly enjoyable was a talented professor who had authored many classic books in my field. He had missed his calling—he should have been a stand-up comic in Las Vegas. We would leave his graduate classes in pain from having laughed so hard at his wonderful Jonathan Winters–style imitations. Unfortunately, he relied so heavily on humor to carry his content that often there was far more laughter than learning.

The motivator

"You can do anything if you simply put your mind to it."

This "pump 'em up and send 'em out" style confuses excitement, which quickly dissipates, with long-term motivation. Learning and performance depend on the protégé's understanding and acceptance of the whys.

Motivator types are typically skilled at telling great parables and stories to illustrate their points. They can be superb at cheerleading—and, indeed, a certain amount of inspiration lends encouragement. Too much, however, gives a false sense of security, the hot air escapes, and nothing remains to help the protégé perform.

The sergeant

"Tell 'em what you're gonna tell 'em. Tell 'em. Then tell 'em what you told 'em."

The sergeant style assumes that protégés are dense and don't want to learn in the first place. Such an assumption is often self-fulfilling. This style also relies on emotional distance, stern discipline, and commanding communication. Sergeants often get movement without motivation. Compliance is mistaken for commitment.

Sergeant Duckett was the drill sergeant in my army basic training company. He was tough and mean and had a megaphone voice that could reduce a private E-nothing recruit to small blobs of jelly. During my last week of boot camp, I needed special permission from Sergeant Duckett to go see the battalion commander. I hardly slept the night before; I tossed and turned, practicing my words. The next morning I entered his office with great trepidation. Instead of the storm trooper from hell, I found a sensitive, compassionate, and surprisingly wise professional. It was my first glimpse of the superb mentor behind his chevrons and medals. What would my infantry training have been like if I had found this resource during my first week instead of my last?

The partner

"You are responsible for your own learning. I am responsible for supporting, facilitating, and learning with you."

The partner role is obviously the one that best serves the protégé and the learning process. We will be exploring the qualities of the partnership-centered mentor in greater depth.

A few of the above assumptions may be a bit overstated. The point, however, is still valid: When we are mentoring, our assumptions affect protégés and may actually impede their learning.

AXIOMS OF LEARNING

Any time a mentor enters into a mentoring relationship, the roles played and the actions taken are grounded in certain assumptions about how people learn. For example, the mentor who believes protégés are like empty vessels waiting to be filled will use an information-dissemination approach, trying to fill the head of the protégé with facts and figures; the mentor who assumes the protégé will resist will tend toward the sergeant approach in an attempt to intimidate.

> **66***The first problem for all of us, men and women, is not to learn, but to unlearn.***99**
>
> — Gloria Steinem

Managers As Mentors is based on five axioms about how adult learning occurs. These concepts were first articulated by my friend Dr. Malcolm Knowles, professor emeritus of adult education at North Carolina State University. Malcolm labeled these axioms *andragogy,* or the practice of adult learning, which he differentiated from *pedagogy,* the practice of child learning.

1. Adults are motivated to learn as they develop needs and interests that learning will satisfy. Therefore, protégés' needs and interests are the appropriate starting points for mentoring.

2. Adult orientation to learning is life- or work-centered. Therefore, the appropriate frameworks for organizing mentoring are life- and/or work-related situations, not academic or theoretical subjects.

3. Experience is the richest resource for adult learning. Therefore, the approach for mentoring involves active

participation in a planned series of experiences, the analysis of those experiences, and their application to work and life situations.

4. Adults have a deep need to be self-directing. Therefore, the role of the mentor is to engage in a process of inquiry, analysis, and decision making with the protégé, rather than to transmit knowledge and then evaluate the protégé's conformity to it.

5. Individual differences among adult learners increase with age and experience. Therefore, mentoring must make optimum provision for differences in style, time, place, and pace of learning.

Perhaps the most important conclusion in considering and adopting these axioms is that the protégé is primarily in charge of his own learning. Mentors do not have the power to implant ideas or to transfer skills directly to the protégé. Mentors can only suggest and guide. The mentor's primary responsibility is to do a good job of managing the relationship through which protégés learn.

QUALITIES OF GREAT MENTORING PARTNERSHIPS

We can identify several qualities that are important in establishing and maintaining a good mentor-protégé partnership:

Balance

If there is a single dimension that separates the andragogy of the future from the pedagogy of the past, it is balance. Unlike a relationship based on power and control, a learning partnership is a balanced alliance grounded in mutuality, interdependence, and respect. Power-seeking mentors tend to mentor with credentials and sovereignty; partnership-driven mentors seek to mentor with authenticity and openness. In a balanced learning partnership, energy is given early in the relationship to role clarity and communication of expectations; there is a spirit of generosity and acceptance rather than a focus on rules and rights. Partners recognize their differences while respecting their common needs and objectives.

Truth

Countless books extol the benefits of clear and accurate communication. Partnership communication has one additional quality—it is clean, pure, characterized by the highest level of integrity and honesty. Truth-seekers work not only to ensure that their words are pure (the truth and nothing but the truth), but also to help others communicate with equal purity. When a mentor works hard to give feedback to a protégé in a way that is caringly frank and compassionately straightforward, it is in pursuit of clean communication. When a mentor implores the protégé for candid feedback, it is a plea for clean communication. The path of learning begins with the mentor's genuineness and candor.

Trust

Trust begins with experience; experience begins with a leap of faith. Perfect monologues, even with airtight proof and solid support documentation, do not foster a climate of experimentation and risk taking. They foster passive acceptance, not personal investment. If protégés see their mentors taking risks, they will follow suit. A trust-full partnership is one in which error is accepted as a necessary step on the path from novice to master.

Abundance

Partnership-driven mentors exude generosity. There is a giver orientation that finds enchantment in sharing wisdom. As Malcolm Knowles says, "Great trainers [and mentors] love learning and are happiest when they are around its occurrence." A partnership grounded in abundance is one between people who never take each other for granted. Such relation-

The preamble to learning is risk. The preamble to risk is courage.

ships are celebratory and affirming. As the mentor gives, the protégé reciprocates, and abundance begins to characterize the relationship.

Passion

Great mentoring partnerships are filled with passion; they are guided by mentors with deep feelings and a willingness to communicate those feelings. Passionate mentors recognize that effective learning has a vitality about it that is not logical, or rational, or orderly. Such mentors get carried away with the spirit of the partnership and their feelings about the process of learning. Some may exude emotion quietly, but their cause-driven energy is clearly present. In a nutshell, mentors not only love the learning process, they love what the protégé can become—and they passionately demonstrate that devotion.

Courage

Mentoring takes courage; learning takes courage. Great mentors are allies of courage; they cultivate a partnership of courageousness. They take risks with learning, showing boldness in their efforts, and elicit courage in protégés by the examples they set. The preamble to learning is risk, the willingness to take a shaky step without the security of perfection. The preamble to risk is courage.

Partnerships are the expectancy of the best in our abilities, attitudes, and aspirations. In a learning partnership, the mentor is not only helping the protégé but continually communicating a belief that he is a fan of the learner. Partnerships are far more than good synergy. Great partnerships go beyond "greater than" to a realm of unforeseen worth. And worth in a mentoring partnership is laced with the equity of balance, the clarity of truth, the security of trust, the affirmation of abundance, the energy of passion, and the boldness of courage.

4

MENTORING IN ACTION

A Continuing Case

ACK GAMBLE was the consummate outdoorsman. Every deer, dove, hog, quail, turkey, and largemouth bass was in grave danger whenever Jack entered the wild with his rifle, shotgun, bow, or reel. But at Gracie-Omar, Inc., he was the consummate mentor.

Gamble was the manufacturing engineering manager at the Triplin, Georgia, plant of Gracie-Omar, a large computer-systems and components plant. He had done his time in the trenches and had quickly worked his way up the chain. Now he reported directly to the plant manager. Jack's upward mobility was due not only to his superior performance and down-home humor but to his unique way of communicating to associates what he learned. As the plant expanded, the plant manager promoted Jack repeatedly, seeing him as the prototype of a "learning organization leader."

Tracy Black was a new systems engineer transferred to Gracie-Omar's Triplin plant from their plant north of Boston. Tracy would ultimately be assigned to Jack. Tracy had nothing in common with Jack, except hunting. Tracy was from upstate New York; Jack was local, born and raised twenty-five miles from Triplin. Tracy had a somber and clipped style; Jack had a mile-wide smile and a drawl as slow as molasses. Tracy was a liberal Republican and Catholic; Jack was a deacon in the Baptist church and a conservative Democrat. Not least, Tracy was a woman; Jack was not.

Tracy and Jack first met at the company picnic. It was Tracy's second day. She arrived thirty minutes late. The only people she knew were the human resources director who had interviewed her, and Rod, the plant manager, whom she had briefly met. The crowd seemed very cliquish to her, their boisterous conversation like code: "We're all big buddies here, and if you're not one of us now, you won't be in this lifetime!" The meeting planner announced how the meal would be served, the plant manager made a short speech, and Jack told a long joke about a mule. The crowd laughed and cheered; she didn't understand what was funny about the punch line. She thought of Boston.

"Howdy," said someone behind her as she was reaching for a short ear of corn in a long serving line. Startled, she quickly turned. "I'm Jack Gamble. Rod tells me you and I will be working together."

Oh, no! she thought privately, Not the mule man! But she managed to utter a crisp "Hello."

Jack asked her the usual fair-weather, cocktail-party questions—where ya from, where'd ya go to school, what'd ya do before you came here, ya wanta sit? At the end of five minutes, Jack suggested that Tracy stop by his office on Monday right after lunch.

Jack's office revealed few clues about its occupant. As Tracy waited there for him to return from a luncheon meeting, she searched for clues about this man who would be her boss and mentor. On the desk was a picture of Jack's wife and two children; on the wall, a framed ISO-9000 certificate and a picture of two wild turkeys. On the floor behind the desk was a piece of equipment that looked like a large blue jug. Other than that, the office could have belonged to anyone.

"Sorry I'm late!" she heard from behind her. "Would you like a glass of real good homemade iced tea?" he asked with the same impish style he had used to tell the mule joke.

"No," said Tracy, more brusquely than she had intended.

Jack served himself from the large blue jug. He continued, warmth and confidence in his words. "Tracy, I'm real excited about getting to work with you. Sarah, over in human resources, tells me you are one terrific systems engineer."

Tracy didn't know how to respond, but Jack continued, not seeming to want a response from her yet.

"You've worked on the LWB-211, which I would really like to know more about. We haven't gotten any of those in here yet, but we plan to in the fourth quarter.

"Now, how can I help you get settled in?" Tracy was not sure, but she asked Jack whether she would be getting a laptop computer with a modem that would enable her to link into the company system when she worked on the road.

"That's a new one," said Jack, writing it on a small pad. "I'll find out and let you know right away. I've been keeping a list of the questions new people ask, along with the answers. I've made you a copy. But the modem question won't be in this issue!" Tracy was beginning to feel more comfortable with Jack.

"I don't know what you think of this plant," Jack went on, "but I sure do remember what I felt. It seemed like a tight family that didn't want any more cousins! I remember feeling downright scared and wondering if I'd made a bum decision. But I made up my mind I wasn't going to let it beat me. I just started acting like I was already in the family. And you know what? It worked like a thirty-ought-six on an eight-pointer at twenty yards!"

Tracy was surprised. "You're a hunter?" she asked.

Jack's eyes twinkled mischievously. He looked like someone who had been caught with his hand in the cookie jar. "You bet!" he said. "And if you aren't, then I just messed in my nest—using an expression that only another hunter would get."

"I hunt, too," replied Tracy, somewhat relieved to have one thing in common with this slow-talking foreigner.

"Terrific!" said Jack. "Do you like to hunt deer?"

Tracy nodded. "I hunt anything in season," she said. It was her first foray into Southern mores.

Jack leaned forward. "That's great! Have you seen the new issue of *Field and Stream*?" She had not. "Well, I have it right here. Why don't you take it? There's a great article on deer stands—has some crazy ideas I plan to try next time my son and I go deer hunting." The two of them continued to talk for some time on their new-found common interest.

> **66***A successful career will no longer be about promotion. It will be about mastery.***99**
>
> — Michael Hammer

A few weeks after Jack and Tracy's get-acquainted meeting, an Ulmer-1911 machine was delivered. Jack had been Ulmer qualified for a few years and had gone back to Wisconsin twice for refresher training. Tracy had heard about but never operated the machine and was eager to learn. Late one afternoon Jack and Tracy sat down for the first time at the 1911's console.

"Before we start," Jack began, "I want to find out what you know about this machine." He listened as Tracy described the machine's purpose and what it could produce. "I see you've done your homework," he said proudly. Tracy smiled.

Jack continued: "Think of this machine as an extension of your right arm and imagine what it would feel like to have that arm ten feet longer than the other. Not only does hand-eye coordination change, but you're bound to feel awkward. Expect that same sensation with the Ulmer-1911."

Tracy began to feel a bit less apprehensive. "Are you going to show me how it works?" she asked, her impatience beginning to show.

"I was just like you," Jack teased, "as anxious as a long-tailed cat in a room full of rocking chairs." Tracy grinned and took a deep breath. "However," Jack added, "it will be better for you to run this machine than to watch me run it. Just looking at the center screen, what do you think is the first step?"

Tracy quickly responded, "I'd say keying on command six and moving the dugen switch to ninety degrees."

"Great choice!" Jack answered. "And what is your objective in taking that route?"

The lesson continued until Tracy was operating the Ulmer fairly proficiently. The only time Jack touched the equipment was after Tracy had taken a series of incorrect steps and gotten so far off the starting point that she needed help in getting back. Jack's goal was to guide her thinking and understanding more than her operating and remembering.

In the months that followed, Jack's and Tracy's relationship improved. Their mutual interest in hunting turned out to be a key source of compatibility. As Tracy grew less nervous and more confident, she began to take more risks in her spirited interaction with Jack. Soon she was matching him jab for friendly jab. She also began assuming greater plant responsibility, including the supervision of four engineers.

One day she stopped Jack in the hall with a look of concern on her face. "Got a few minutes?" she asked.

Five minutes later they were in her office. "Adam's a problem," she began bluntly after Jack closed the door behind him.

She had learned that with Jack there was no need to beat around the bush. "Just cut to the chase," he had encouraged her. It had proven helpful in her dealings with some of the more impatient engineers.

"Tell me more," Jack replied, sitting in the chair in front of her desk.

Adam was one of Tracy's new direct reports. "He's not pulling his weight. I've encouraged him, counseled him, and tried to understand him. I'm running out of patience."

Jack waited to make sure she had no more to say about the subject. "How can I help?" he asked, not wanting to assume anything yet about whether his assistance was required.

Tracy looked straight at him. "I guess I need you to be a sounding board, and maybe give me some ideas on how to get him fired up—or fired."

"What do you think the problem is, based on what you know?" asked Jack.

"His morale is lousy. When I try to talk with him about his performance, his nonverbals are rather patronizing, like he's offended that I raised the issue."

Jack thought for a minute. "I can see that would be a tough nut to crack. I've never been really comfortable dealing with negative performers. It always makes me feel anxious if I have to get tough with an employee. I can see—"

"But you still manage to get them turned around," interrupted Tracy.

Jack could see that Tracy thought he had some magical secret he had kept to himself. "You believe there's a special technique that maybe you've missed."

"Yes, I suppose I do, in a way. You make it look easy. I remember when you had to terminate Edsel Joiner. The guy ended up thanking you for it!"

Jack did not respond for a while. Tracy suddenly felt awkward, as though she had allowed her stream of emotion to overflow its banks. Then, with unusual emotion in his voice, Jack said, "That was the scariest thing I've done since I came to work here." They both sat in silence.

Jack took another stab at the issue. "How does he react when you get stern and serious?"

"I'm not sure," Tracy responded.

Jack tried again. "Let me ask it this way: If I asked Adam to candidly describe you when the two of you talk about his performance, what words would he use?"

Tracy's demeanor began to change. It was as if the wheels of wisdom were turning in her head.

"He would say I was relentlessly patient." She was still half lost in thought.

"What else?"

Tracy responded with near excitement in her voice. "He would *not* describe me as tough, demanding, or disciplined."

Jack sensed that she was solving her own issue. Again, he paused before raising another question. He knew instinctively

> **66***N*othing** ever becomes real till it is experienced. Even a proverb is no proverb to you till your life has illustrated it. **99**
>
> —John Keats

that pace was everything when insight was the goal. "So, what do you think should be your next step?"

Tracy began to outline steps: a serious conversation, a performance plan, short-term goals with clear feedback, supervision with a shorter leash, and, above all, less understanding and more discipline. Jack offered a few ideas, but mostly affirmation and encouragement. They parted with an agreement to revisit the issue in a few days.

The story had a happy ending. Adam admitted to Tracy that he was having difficulty working for a woman but ultimately grew to respect her, turning out excellent performance. Tracy was promoted to department manager, then transferred to corporate headquarters in Wisconsin. Jack mentored more new engineers. He was offered promotions but turned down those that involved a move. Woods for hunting were more important than mahogany row. Besides, he got a kick out watching people learn—especially those who weren't sure they were going to fit in.

ASSESSING YOUR MENTORING TALENTS

5

A Self-Check Scale

ELF-ASSESSMENT: does the term make you think of navel gazing? Perhaps you've had enough of the joys of testing, performance reviews, exams, and the like. Seems more about masochism than mastery! However, drawing a finer bead on our gifts and blind spots can be a helpful preamble to improvement and growth—and that, after all, is what mentoring is all about.

The goal of the Mentor Scale is to provide a painless way to determine what personal attributes you bring to the mentoring relationship. The goal is not to judge, evaluate, or criticize you as a person; there are no right or wrong answers. The objective is to offer you a picture of your gifts and your potential blind spots. For example, if I know I have a tendency to procrastinate, I can take steps to counter that tendency, to break the habit of putting things off until the last minute.

At this point, you may be thinking of zipping on past this chapter. Please resist the temptation. I encourage you to take the instrument. There will be many references to it throughout the rest of the book. If you haven't done the self-assessment, you will miss out on some potential mentoring insights. You do not have to put your answers in the book; simply write them on a separate sheet of paper. This way you can easily review your answers as we revisit the Mentor Scale at various points throughout the book.

Now, pencils ready? Here goes . . .

THE TEST

On the following pages are listed thirty-nine sentence stems, each with two possible endings. Keeping your work environment in mind, quickly review each item and circle the letter of the ending that best completes the sentence. Read each item carefully, but choose your response quickly. Instruments like this tend to be more accurate if you go with your immediate reaction rather than pondering your choice. Do not leave items blank. You will find some items in which neither choice is perfectly accurate; select the one that seems better. After completing the inventory, proceed to the scoring sheet.

The Mentor Scale

1. People probably see me as   a. a soft touch   b. hard nosed

2. Workdays I like the most are   a. unpredictable   b. planned

3. When it comes to celebrations,
   most organizations need   a. fewer   b. more

4. When I evaluate people, my
   decisions are based on   a. mercy   b. justice

5. My approach to planning my
   personal activities is   a. easygoing   b. orderly

6. People generally see me as
   a person who is   a. formal   b. personable

7. When it comes to social
   situations, I tend to   a. hold back   b. jump in

8. I like to spend my leisure
   time in ways that are fairly   a. spontaneous   b. routine

9. I believe leaders should
   be more concerned about
   employee   a. rights   b. feelings

10. When I encounter people
    in need of help, I'm more
    likely to   a. avoid   b. pitch in

11. When I am in a group,
    I typically   a. follow   b. lead

12. Most people see me as   a. private   b. open

13. My friends know that I am   a. gentle   b. firm

14. If I were in a group of strangers,
    people would most likely
    remember me as a   a. listener   b. leader

15. When it comes to expressing
    my feelings, most people
    probably see me as   a. guarded   b. comfortable

16. When people I depend on make
    mistakes, I am typically   a. patient   b. impatient

17. When I eat out, I generally order food that — a. sounds unique — b. I know I like

18. In general, I prefer — a. the theater — b. a party

19. In a conflict, when anger is involved, my emotional fuse is usually — a. long — b. short

20. In an emergency situation, I would likely be — a. calm — b. anxious

21. I prefer to express myself to others in ways that are — a. indirect — b. direct

22. I am likely to be ruled by — a. emotion — b. logic

23. When in new and unfamiliar situations, I am usually — a. carefree — b. careful

24. In a festive social situation, I am usually — a. passive — b. active

25. When I am blamed for something I did not cause, my initial reaction is to — a. listen — b. defend

26. If I am in a situation in which I lose or am left disappointed, I get — a. sad — b. mad

27. If someone came to me in tears, I would probably feel — a. awkward — b. at home

28. Most people see me as — a. an optimist — b. a pessimist

29. People usually see me as — a. uncritical — b. critical

30. If people were given a forced choice, they would say I was — a. too quiet — b. too loud

31. At the end of a long party, I usually find myself — a. exhausted — b. energized

32. When I work on projects, I am best at getting them — a. started — b. completed

33. I believe people should approach their work with — a. dedication — b. inspiration

34. My social blunders typically
    leave me   a. embarrassed   b. amused

35. When my organization
    announces a major change,
    I get   a. excited   b. concerned

36. People are likely to see
    me as   a. firm   b. warm

37. After a tough day, I like
    to unwind   a. alone   b. with others

38. Change is most often your   a. friend   b. adversary

39. My work and social life   a. are separate   b. often
                                                            overlap

---

The Scoring Form

Sociability

Using simple hash marks, tally your A's and B's for the 13 sociability items.

		A's	*B's*
1, 4, 7, 10, 13, 16, 19,			
22, 25, 28, 31, 34, 37	Totals	_____	_____

Dominance

Do the same for the 13 dominance items . . .

		A's	*B's*
2, 5, 8, 11, 14, 17, 20,			
23, 26, 29, 32, 35, 38	Totals	_____	_____

Openness

. . . and for the 13 openness items.

		A's	*B's*
3, 6, 9, 12, 15, 18, 21,			
24, 27, 30, 33, 36, 39	Totals	_____	_____

INTERPRETATION

The Mentor Scale is inspired by the FIRO-B®, an excellent instrument developed by Will Schutz and distributed exclusively by Consulting Psychologists Press. The scale measures—at one point in time—a mentor's need for sociability, dominance, and openness, all crucial components of an effective mentoring relationship. (Shultz's FIRO-B® instrument labels these components "inclusion," "control," and "affection," respectively.)

Sociability has to do with your preference for being with or apart from others. People with high column-A scores in sociability tend to be reserved loners; those with high column-B scores tend to be outgoing joiners. People with similar numbers of A's and B's are neither highly sociable nor highly reserved; they can be moderately sociable or moderately reserved, depending on the situation.

What does sociability have to do with mentoring? People who have high sociability scores will find the rapport-building and dialogue-leading dimensions of mentoring easier. They will have to work hard to avoid dominating discussions. Low sociability scores are found among people whose reserve may make them a bit unapproachable. These people will need to work harder at helping protégés open up and communicate.

Dominance is about your preference regarding being in charge. People with high column-A scores are comfortable having someone else do the leading, and often prefer it. People with high column-B scores tend to like being in control and often assert that need. Low dominance scores can also indicate a high need for independence. People with balanced scores are neither highly dominant nor highly submissive. They can control moderately or not at all, depending on the situation.

Dominance is a major issue in mentoring with a partnering philosophy. The whole concept of mentoring today is based on a relationship of shared power. High dominance scorers are reluctant either to give up control or to share control of the relationship; they have to work hard to listen rather than talk. Low dominance scorers, on the other hand, may need to work to assume leadership of the relationship. They may take such a low-key, laissez-faire approach that the protégé feels insecure and without guidance.

> **66***You never find yourself until you face the truth.***99**
>
> — Pearl Bailey

Openness refers to how easily you trust others. High column-A scores are found among people who are cautious, guarded, and reluctant to show feelings. High column-B scores are typical of people with many close relationships, who are comfortable being vulnerable and tend to express their feelings easily. People with similar A and B scores are moderately open or moderately cautious, depending on the situation.

High openness scorers will find it easy to reveal themselves in a mentoring relationship. In fact, their challenge is to be candid and open enough to encourage the protégé to do likewise, while not being so aggressive as to overwhelm or intimidate the protégé. Low openness scorers, however, will need to work at overcoming their caution in order to take early emotional and interpersonal risks with the protégé; their instinctive guardedness can make the protégé feel that mistakes might have dire consequences.

Several chapters ahead have sidebars addressing the implications of your Mentor Scale scores in terms of each chapter's issues and challenges. The goal is to show you how to use your strengths and compensate for your weaknesses. Can one be too sociable or too open? Of course! Is it not important in some situations to be highly dominant? Again, of course! For effective mentoring, however, my view is that you push toward the high side of sociability and openness, toward the low side of dominance. For interpretations of the sidebars found on pages 72–73, 114–115, and 126, we will consider high column-A scores to be *low* sociability, dominance, or openness and high column-B scores to be *high* sociability, dominance, or openness.

Remember, the Mentor Scale gives you a reading at a moment in time, one that may change with the circumstances. Keep in mind also that the scale assesses only three aspects of your leadership personality. Don't generalize the results beyond their intent; too often, personality instruments are used to label or categorize people, to discount their individual uniqueness. Learn from the Mentor Scale—but avoid using the results as though they were holy writ.

PART

II

SURRENDERING

*L*uke Skywalker is stranded on a strange planet, his spaceship submerged deep in sludge. His only company is his mentor, Yoda, the Jedi warrior. The tiny, strange-looking creature encourages Luke to use the force. "I'll try," replies a discouraged, exhausted Luke.

"No. Try not. Do, or do not," retorts Yoda. "There is no try."

All fans of The Empire Strikes Back *know how this scene ends. After Luke gives up, Yoda, using some strange connection with a universal energy field, wills the spaceship out of the bog and onto dry land. Although this is just movie magic, every person in the theater has a strange identification with Yoda's action.*

The force behind Yoda's action goes by many names. An artist refers to it as "the muse." Surfers call it "flow"; others call it "being in the groove" or "being on." Call it what you may, the feeling is unmistakable.

There is a similar moment in a mentoring relationship when everything clicks and a spirit or force seems to lift the connection to a level of purity, of unspoken understanding. Wisdom, insight, and growth burst from these moments. Learning happens at warp speed. We seem surprisingly clear and uniquely receptive to understanding. This is mentoring at its best.

How does this high-octane learning occur? What action does the mentor need to take to encourage this synergistic moment with a protégé? In a word, surrender. *The magical first step is to surrender to the process.*

Surrendering means completely relinquishing any effort to control or manipulate the outcome. Surrendering means putting all effort into being completely authentic, real, and mask-free. Surrendering means being devoted to learning, not dedicated to convincing. As management consultant Bruce Fritch says, "Surrendering is the most difficult and most courageous interpersonal act a leader can take with a subordinate. It is also the most powerful!"

Years ago I worked with Dr. Richard Furr, a gifted consulting psychologist. He and I designed and taught a series of executive workshops on performance coaching. The final advice Richard gave attendees was to practice their newfound skills on a couple of subordinates within the coming week.

"Start with practice," he would say, "by telling your associates something like the following: 'I have just attended a workshop on performance coaching and learned some new skills I want to use in our relationship. I will be very awkward at first and make a lot of mistakes. But with some practice and your

patience, I will get better. And we will both benefit.'"

The advice was a valuable relationship builder. Attendees at follow-up sessions reported enormous success. The authenticity caused subordinates to see their leaders in a new light. Many reported that their sessions with subordinates turned out to be the single most powerful and productive conversation they had ever had. The typical executive report went something like this: "When I gave up trying to force it to work, it seemed to take on a life of its own and steered the relationship where it needed to go. It was amazing. I have never felt anything like it. It was like magic." This like-magic quality of mentoring begins to happen with surrendering.

KINDLING KINSHIP

The Power of Rapport

E BEGIN LIFE with a bond: infant and mother. Life, for most of us, does not start with anxiety or fear. Life begins with security and trust. The path from dependence to independence teaches us about rejection, discomfort, and pain. We begin to protect ourselves with the shield of personality (the Greek word for "personality" means "mask") and assume that each new relationship is a threat until shown otherwise. The ritual of relationship is the gradual lowering of the mask.

"Rapport" comes from an old French word that means "a bringing back" or "harmony renewed." This definition reminds us that rapport is fundamentally about actions aimed at restoring the security of our initial bond.

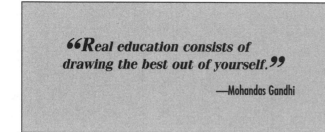

"Real education consists of drawing the best out of yourself."

—Mohandas Gandhi

The success of a mentoring relationship can hang on the first encounters between mentor and protégé. The tone set in the first meeting can decide whether the relationship will be fruitful or fraught with fear and anxiety. Rapport building expedites shield lowering; quality learning will not occur until the shield has been lowered enough for the learner to take risks in front of the mentor. As the person who is usually in the driver's seat at the outset of the relationship, the mentor must ensure a good start—the renewal of the original bond.

Can a mentoring relationship get back on track if the first encounter falters? Of course—and thank goodness. Most of us can remember a solid friendship that started out on shaky ground. We also remember how long it took and how much energy had to be expended to overcome that rocky beginning. But the sooner we can establish rapport, the more time and energy we save; and the sooner the relationship moves onto solid ground, the faster learning can occur. The old Southern custom of bringing a gift when visiting a friend, telling a funny story to open a speech, or making small talk to kick off a sales call all acknowledge that openings are potentially rocky *and* important.

THE COMPONENTS OF RAPPORT

What does rapport building entail for a mentor? How does the mentor establish early kinship, trust, and comfort? Here is some insight to the four components of rapport: leveling communications, gifting gestures, receptivity for feelings, and reflective responses. (Okay, there are probably twenty-five components—or twenty-five hundred—but in this book we will work with four. We all know there is not a finite number of most things, especially in areas like habits, wonders of the world, ways to leave your lover, or components of rapport. The four here were chosen for convenience and workability.) Find your own techniques consistent with the components. To jump start your efforts, I've included several applications in each section.

Leveling communication

Rapport begins with the sounds and sights of openness and positive regard. Any normal person approaching a potentially anxious encounter will raise his antennae high in search of clues about the road ahead: Will this situation embarrass me? Will this person take advantage of me? Will I be effective in this encounter? Is there harm awaiting me?

Given the protégé's search for early warning signs, the mentor must be quick to transmit signals of welcome. An open posture (for example, no crossed arms), warm and enthusiastic gestures, eye contact, removing physical barriers, and personalized greetings all communicate a desire for a level playing field. Mentors who broadcast power signals (peering over an imposing desk, making the protégé do all the approaching, tight and closed body language, a reserved manner, or facial expressions that telegraph distance) risk complete failure to establish a good mentoring partnership.

Quality learning will not occur until the shield has been lowered enough for the learner to take risks in front of the mentor.

Gifting gestures

The opening communication can signal only that the path ahead may be safe for travel; it does not ensure rapport. The "Actions speak louder than words" adage is uniquely fitting at this juncture. Protégés need a gesture or action that they can take as a token of affinity.

Establishing rapport is a bit like courtship. You don't say, "Hi, I'm Bill. Let's get married. How's tomorrow at three?"

There's a little matter of dating, gifts, parties, meeting the family, showers, ministers—all the preliminaries needed for a long-lasting and rewarding relationship.

The best mentors are especially creative to this purpose. The perfunctory "How about a cup of coffee?" is certainly a well-worn gifting gesture. However, think about how much more powerful a statement like "I had my assistant locate this article I thought you might find useful" could be as early evidence that the relationship will be a friendly one. I once had a mentor who kept a supply of his wife's homemade jellies for visitors. The gift was always bestowed early in the encounter, not at the end.

There are as many ways to signal benign intent as there are mentors and protégés. Find one that suits you and works for your associates.

Receptivity for feelings

The late, great psychologist Carl Rogers wrote extensively on unconditional positive regard and its impact on the relationship. His research repeatedly affirmed the role such a generous attitude had on psychological healing and wellness. A good mentor establishes rapport through careful attentiveness to the protégé's feelings early in the encounter. When people believe they are heard and understood, they feel secure and comfortable. Establishing rapport is not about asking, "How are you feeling?" It is about listening intently to ascertain the feelings behind the words—and (as we will see in chapter 10) making responses that acknowledge these feelings.

Patricia Sellers, in her article "What Exactly Is Charisma?", profiles Orit Gadiesh, the chair of the prestigious consulting firm Bain & Company. "Orit has that talent for making you feel you're the most important person in the room. She bleeds your blood." One way she makes clients feel important, reports Sellers, is by never looking at her watch. Inside Bain, Gadiesh has long been regarded as a junior consultant's most generous mentor.

In her story "Mockingbirds," Mary Oliver tells of an elderly couple visited by strangers in their poor abode. Lacking

A good mentor establishes rapport through careful attentiveness to the protégé's feelings early in the encounter.

any goods to offer their visitors, the couple simply listen to their guests with all their heart. The strangers turn out to be gods who view the couple's attentiveness as the very best gift humans can give. Gods and protégés are moved and mellowed by mentors who listen from the heart. As a mentor, continually ask yourself, "What must she be feeling right now? How might I feel if our roles were reversed?"

Reflective responses

Receptivity to the protégé's feelings enables you to provide a tailor-made reflective response that says, "I've been there as well." This gesture, another way of saying, "I am the same as you," promotes the kinship and closeness that are vital to trust. The goal is empathetic identification. Empathy is different from sympathy. The word "sympathy" comes from the Greek word *synpatheia,* meaning "shared feeling." Empathy means "in-feeling," or the ability to understand another's feelings. Relationship strength is not spawned by "Misery loves company"; it comes through "I've been there too" identification.

Reflective responses can be as simple as a short personal story that lets the protégé know that you appreciate his feelings. Mildly self-deprecating anecdotes can work well, too. Above all, rapport is best served by humility and sensitivity. If you feel awkward, say you do. If you feel excited, say so. The sooner you speak your feelings, the faster the protégé will match your vulnerability.

These ideas about rapport can provide guidance in this important getting-started phase of mentoring. However, you should also keep in mind that the main ingredient in the recipe for rapport is authenticity. The more you surrender to who you are in front of the protégé, the more at home she will feel. Compatibility is as vital in coaching as in any other important relationship. How quickly and effectively that compatibility is established can make a major difference in how competent the protégé becomes.

The main ingredient in the recipe for rapport is authenticity. The more you surrender to who you are in front of the protégé, the more at home she will feel.

Jack Gamble on Rapport
("Mentoring in Action" Revisited)

Sorry I'm late!" she heard from behind her. "Would you like a glass of real good homemade iced tea?" he asked with the same impish style he had used to tell the mule joke.

"No," said Tracy, more brusquely than she had intended.

Jack served himself from the large blue jug. He continued, warmth and confidence in his words. "Tracy, I'm real excited about getting to work with you. Sarah, over in human resources, tells me you are one terrific systems engineer." Tracy didn't know how to respond, but Jack continued, not seeming to want a response from her yet. "You've worked on the LWB-211, which I would really like to know more about. We haven't gotten any of those in here yet, but we plan to in the fourth quarter.

"Now, how can I help you get settled in?" Tracy was not sure, but she asked Jack whether she would be getting a laptop computer with a modem that would enable her to link into the company system when she worked on the road.

"That's a new one," said Jack, writing it on a small pad. "I'll find out and let you know right away. I've been keeping a list of the questions new people ask, along with the answers. I've made you a copy. But the modem question won't be in this issue!" Tracy was beginning to feel more comfortable with Jack.

"I don't know what you think of this plant," Jack went on, "but I sure do remember what I felt. It seemed like a tight family that didn't want any more cousins! I remember feeling downright scared and wondering if I'd made a bum decision. But I made up my mind I wasn't going to let it beat me. I just started acting like I was already in the family. And you know what? It worked like a thirty-ought-six on an eight-pointer at twenty yards!"

Tracy was surprised. "You're a hunter?" she asked.

Jack's eyes twinkled mischievously. He looked like someone who had been caught with his hand in the cookie jar. "You bet!" he said. "And if you aren't, then I just messed in my nest—using an expression that only another hunter would get."

"I hunt, too," replied Tracy, somewhat relieved to have one thing in common with this slow-talking foreigner.

"Terrific!" said Jack. "Do you like to hunt deer?"

Tracy nodded. "I hunt anything in season," she said. It was her first foray into Southern mores.

Jack leaned forward. "That's great! Have you seen the new issue of Field and Stream?" She had not. "Well, I have it right here. Why don't you take it? There's a great article on deer stands—has some crazy ideas I plan to try next time my son and I go deer hunting." The two of them continued to talk for some time on their newfound common interest.

7

AVOIDING THIN ICE

Advice and Feedback

SOMEONE once asked famed Notre Dame head football coach Lou Holtz what he considered to be the toughest part of his job. With his typical "aw shucks" charm, he finessed the question but ultimately communicated that one of the hardest parts was "teaching lessons that stay taught." Mentors have a similar challenge.

Mentoring can involve everything from chalkboard teaching to spirited discussion to circulation of relevant articles, but one of its most challenging parts is giving advice and feedback. Recall the last time someone said, "Let me give you a little advice [feedback]!" No doubt it quickly put you into a defensive posture. Psychologists remind us that we all have authority hangups of varying severity. So does your protégé—and the protégé's resistance to advice and resentment of feedback create the challenge in teaching lessons that stay taught. As one frustrated supervisor commented, "I tell 'em what they ought to do, but it seems to go in one ear and out the other!"

GIVING ADVICE WITHOUT GETTING RESISTANCE

Advice giving works only in the context of learning—that is, when you are offering advice because you believe that the protégé's performance will be improved if her knowledge or skill is enhanced. This is important, because for advice giving truly to work, you must be ready for the protégé to choose *not* to take your advice. If the protégé has no real choice about honoring your advice, then you should simply give a directive and be done with it. Couching your requirement as advice is manipulative and will only foster distrust and resentment.

Below are four steps to make your advice giving more powerful and more productive. The steps are numbered because the sequence is crucial to your success.

For advice giving truly to work, you must be ready for the protégé to choose not to take your advice.

Step 1: Clearly state the performance problem or goal

Begin your advice giving by letting the protégé know the focus or intent of your mentoring. Suppose you're offering advice about improving the performance of a new skill the protégé is trying to master. You might say, "George, I wanted to talk with you about the fact that although your last quarter call rate was up, your sales were down 20 percent." For advice giving to work, you must be very specific and clear in your statement. Ambiguity clouds the conversation and risks leaving the protégé more confused than enlightened.

Stating the focus—an important coaching technique in general—helps sort out the form and content of the advice. Is the problem something that is not working or something that is lacking? Stated differently, is the occasion for the advice a skill deficiency (requiring mentoring) or a will deficiency (requiring coaching)? Being clear up front about the purpose of your advice can help focus your scattergun thoughts into laserlike advice.

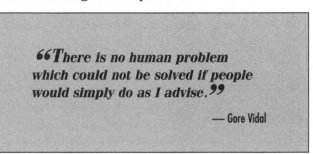

66There is no human problem which could not be solved if people would simply do as I advise.99

— Gore Vidal

Step 2: Make sure you agree on the focus

If what seems to you a performance challenge is seen by the protégé as something else, your advice will be viewed as over-controlling or smothering. Make sure the protégé is as eager to improve as you are to see him improve. You may learn that the protégé has already determined what to do and has little need for your advice. Your goal is to hear the protégé say something like, "Yes, I've been concerned about that as well."

What do you do if you think there is something the protégé needs to learn but the protégé is unwilling? Many lessons get "taught" (but not learned) under this scenario. As Abraham Lincoln said, "A person convinced against his will is of the same opinion still."

Take a broader perspective. If a performance deficiency needs to be remedied, have available objective information that you both can examine. If all else fails, wait until the protégé shows more readiness to learn. To abuse the old adage: You can lead a horse to water, but you can't make him think. While protégés are by no means horses, they can sometimes be as stubborn.

Step 3: Ask permission to give advice

This is the most important step. Your goal at this point is twofold: (1) to communicate advice without eliciting protégé resistance, and (2) to keep ownership of the challenge with the protégé. This does not mean asking, "May I have your permission to . . . ?" Rather, "I have some ideas on how you might improve if that would be helpful to you."

I know what you're thinking. What fool is going to tell his boss, "I'm not interested in your advice!"? Most protégés will heed your advice, of course, and many will be grateful for it. But remember, your goal is to communicate in a way that minimizes the protégé's being controlled or coerced—especially her *perception* of being controlled.

The essence of resistance is control. None of us is thrilled to be told what to do, and some are more intransigent than others. So what do you do if, despite your best efforts, you sense protégé resistance?

Two rules: (1) Never resist resistance. Back off; take a second. Examine your stance, tone, choice of words to see if you might be inadvertently fueling the resistance.

Then: (2) Name the issue and take the hit! Sometimes, simply stating in a low-key, nonconfrontational way how you see the situation—while assuming culpability—can drain the tension. You could say something like this: "I could be wrong on this, but I worry that I may have come on too strong just now and implied that I was commanding you. That was not my intent."

Keeping your advice in the first-person singular helps to eliminate the shoulds and ought-tos.

Step 4: State your advice in the first person singular

Phrases like "you ought to" quickly raise resistance! By keeping your advice in the first-person singular—"what *I* found helpful" or "what worked for *me*"—helps eliminate the shoulds and ought-tos. The protégé will hear such advice unscreened by defensiveness or resistance.

A DRAMA IN FOUR STEPS

Now let's put the steps together in a role play to illustrate the tone and technique of advice giving. Tony is a new reservations clerk for Mayday Airlines; Christa is his section leader. Mayday has just installed a new reservation system. Some of the features are similar to the old system, on which Tony was an expert. Some of the steps can be done one of several ways. Christa has observed that Tony follows a mass-pull-sort approach on the new system, as he did on the old. She believes Tony's efficiency would improve if he used a pull-mass-spread-sort approach.

Christa: "Tony, I've been impressed with your work. I've also noticed that your pace seems to slow when you use the mass-pull-sort approach."

Tony: "Yes, I must admit I find that approach a lot more comfortable. I guess using it for ten years has something to do with it."

Christa: "I know exactly what you mean. It was tough for me to let go of some of the older approaches, especially when you're evaluated on speed and you know that shifting to a new approach will slow you down at first. I've been watching how you do it, and I have a suggestion that might help improve your speed over time."

Tony: "Shoot. I'm all ears if it helps me get faster."

Christa: "I found that the pull-mass-spread-sort approach, while awkward at first, gave me a lot more control over the reservation fields and was actually easier after a day or so than mass-pull-sort. I'll be honest with you—if someone had told me it would be easier, I wouldn't have believed it. But I tried it and was really surprised. You might want to try it yourself."

Being clear up front about the purpose of your advice can help focus your scattergun thoughts into laserlike advice.

Tony: "Sounds all right. I'll give it a try."

And they all lived happily ever after, of course.

Giving advice is like playing pinball: only by pushing and pulling can you encourage the ball to go in a new direction and increase your score. But too much pushing and pulling can cause a tilt and stop the game. Effective mentors recognize the challenge of "teaching so it stays taught" and meet that challenge by coupling their wisdom with sensitivity. They keep the ball in play as long as they can by judicious application of pushes and pulls, nudges and bumps, building the score—the protégé's competence.

GIVING FEEDBACK WITHOUT GETTING RESENTMENT

What's the difference between feedback and advice? Advice is about expanding the scope of knowledge; feedback is about filling a blind spot. I'll illustrate with a true-life experience.

In the late '60s I served in Vietnam as an army infantry unit commander in the 82nd Airborne. Attached to my combat unit was an artillery officer who worked as the forward observer (FO) for the artillery unit in the rear that supported our field operations. This FO essentially served as the eyes for the gunner pulling the lanyard on the artillery piece. As rounds were fired several miles out, the FO observed their impact and, using a field radio, called in corrections to improve the accuracy of the next shot.

> **_Advice is like a stranger—if welcome, he stays the night; if not welcome, he returns home that day._**
>
> — African proverb

The FO never said, "Lousy shot," or, "Well, that was better than last week." He would simply say, "Drop one hundred meters," or "West one-fifty," or "Pay dirt!" This was feedback, not advice; the FO had a perspective the gunner needed and did not have.

There is one key difference between artillery feedback and mentoring feedback: artillery feedback is not likely to make the recipient mad. Advice is expertise the protégé may have or could acquire. Resistance to advice is therefore about premature smartness—that is, "You (the mentor) are telling me (the protégé) something you know that, in time, I can learn on my own." But with feedback, the issue is this: "You (the mentor) are telling me something you know that I will never learn on my own, and that irritates me." The issue with advice is potential resistance; with feedback, it is potential resentment.

The issue with advice is potential resistance; with feedback, it is potential resentment.

"But what about confirming feedback?" you may be thinking. "Surely protégés won't resent feedback telling them that their efforts are on target." To the protégé, however, such well-intentioned confirmation can seem patronizing. The unspoken reply to your "This report you wrote is complete and effective" may be "What gives you the right to tell me this?"

For several years I had an acquaintance who was legally blind (today we would call her visually challenged). She was not self-conscious about her challenge. At a dinner party, a close friend asked her, "What is the hardest part about being blind?" She replied, "When people assist me, I sometimes cannot tell if the help is for my preservation or their pretension." Confirming feedback should contain the same level of care as corrective feedback.

How does a mentor bestow a gift that by its nature reminds the protégé of his inability to see it? Below are four steps that can make giving feedback more powerful and more productive. The steps are numbered because the order is vital to their effectiveness.

Step 1: Create a climate of identification ("I'm like you")

A key factor in giving feedback is the protégé's embarrassment over her blind spot. Granted, "embarrassment" might at times

Jack Gamble on Advice Giving
("Mentoring in Action" Revisited)

*J*ack waited to make sure she had no more to say about the subject. "How can I help?" he asked, not wanting to assume anything yet about whether his assistance was required.

Tracy looked straight at him. "I guess I need you to be a sounding board, and maybe give me some ideas on how to get him fired up—or fired."

"What do you think the problem is, based on what you know?" asked Jack.

"His morale is lousy. When I try to talk with him about his performance, his nonverbals are rather patronizing, like he's offended that I raised the issue."

Jack thought for a minute. "I can see that would be a tough nut to crack. I've never been really comfortable dealing with negative performers. It always makes me feel anxious if I have to get tough with an employee. I can see—"

"But you still manage to get them turned around," interrupted Tracy.

Jack could see that Tracy thought he had some magical secret he had kept to himself. "You believe there's a special technique that maybe you've missed."

"Yes, I suppose I do, in a way. You make it look easy. I remember when you had to terminate Edsel Joiner. The guy ended up thanking you for it!"

Jack did not respond for a while. Tracy suddenly felt awkward, as though she had allowed her stream of emotion to overflow its banks. Then, with unusual emotion in his voice, Jack said, "That was the scariest thing I've done since I came to work here." They both sat in silence.

be too strong a label for the protégé's feelings, but at other times it is not strong enough. In any event, the mentor can enhance the protégé's receptivity by creating a climate of identification. Make comments that have an "I'm like you—that is, not perfect or flawless" message. This need not be a major production—just a sentence or two to establish rapport.

Step 2: State the rationale for feedback

In addition to overcoming embarrassment about the blind spot, the protégé will need to understand the context of the feedback. Help the protégé gain a clear sense of why the feedback is being given. Ensure that there is a clear perspective for making sense of the feedback. When you give feedback, you never want to make the protégé wonder, Why is she telling me this? or How in the world can I benefit from this?

Step 3: Assume you're giving yourself the feedback

Besides being clear and empathetic, feedback must be straightforward and honest. This does not mean it must be blunt or cruel; it means that the protégé should not be left wondering, "What did she *not* tell me that I needed to hear?" Trust is born of clean communication. Think of your goal this way: How would you deliver the feedback if you were giving it to yourself? Take your cues from your own preferences; give feedback as you would receive it.

Think of your goal this way: How would you deliver the feedback if you were giving it to yourself?

Step 4: Ask for what you gave—feedback

There is one action you can take that will both help you improve your mentoring and level the playing field in the protégé's mind: ask for feedback from the protégé. Let the protégé know that you want the feedback process to work both ways. From time to time the forward observer attached to my army infantry unit would ask the gunner for feedback on his FO technique. The gunner was given a shot at calling in a few corrections of his own, so to speak. It gave our unit confidence to know that the dialogue was a two-way street.

It is instructive that the word "feedback" starts with the word "feed." Truly the best gap filling happens in the spirit of feeding or nurturing. It is also fitting that the word "advice" probably came from the Latin word "concilium," meaning "to call together." Our words "counsel" and "consult" have the same origin. If we blend these archaic definitions of feedback and advice, we get a perfect description of a learning partnership—"to feed together."

SOCRATES' GREAT SECRET

Awesome Queries

I F THERE WERE a Mentors' Hall of Fame, Socrates would be an instant inductee. In a heated argument over whether virtue could be taught (the ancient Greeks believed that slaves, as uneducated people, could not be truly virtuous), Socrates bet a case of mead (Greek for Bud Light) that he could teach a common slave the Pythagorean theorem (for those who used it in high school and then filed it away: the square of the hypotenuse of a right triangle is equal to the sum of the squares of the other two sides). He had no overhead projector, handouts, or textbook.

He needed only two tools to teach the slave: the capacity to ask the right question and the ability to listen carefully to the meaning behind the answer. To this day the method behind his bold bet is memorialized as Socratic teaching.

> **"It's an unanswered question, but let us still believe in the dignity and importance of the question."**
>
> — Tennessee Williams

Socrates understood the secret of mentoring: effective questioning brings insight, which fuels curiosity, which cultivates wisdom. Now we will examine, methodically and anecdotally, how the Socratic method works. You will learn why Socrates' secret is such a powerful one.

I have a friend who returned from a family reunion in a tiny town in rural South Carolina. He is a prominent surgeon at a major hospital and teaches part time at a prestigious medical school. "I finally realized," he told me, "why I remember my childhood as a painfully boring experience." He took off his reading glasses and momentarily stared into space. "There was no growth, and I was frightened that I might be trapped in a tomb of intellectual stagnation."

At first I thought his assessment seemed too bitter and his reaction arrogant. He went on to describe his early days of living in an imaginary world for weeks at a time just to avoid the monotony of a small-town life in which change was shunned and uniqueness punished. He hid in books because conversations with others offered only shallow and perfunctory mental activity. He talked to his pets, who understood him but couldn't talk back.

His withdrawal into himself opened the way to academic achievement, escape from stagnation, and eventual success. For many years he blamed the pain of his youth on the misfortune of growing up in a boring setting. However, his return to his childhood home gave him new insight. It was not the unstimulating environment but rather the dearth of curiosity that had imprisoned his soul.

"They have great barbecue," he remarked with a smile, describing the weekend reunion. "But they don't ask questions." I prodded him to explain. "People at the reunion talked; there was a lot of conversation. And there was a lot of concerned communication. But no one really interviewed me. Oh, I got quite a few fact-finding questions, but no follow-ups. No one was really curious about my life—only concerned about being polite. I even tried to seed the encounters by working hard to learn about their views, feelings, ideas, joys, and fears. They seemed eager to give me a peek into their souls. But after such a one-sided dialogue, I left South Carolina feeling highly informed about their world, but lonely and again bored."

His sad story made me reflect on the role that questions—real questions, the search for understanding—can play in growth. Quality questions have a multiplier effect on learning. Ask an information-seeking question, you get only an answer or a fact; ask an understanding-seeking question and you unleash a more powerful chain of events. Here's how it works.

Effective questioning brings insight, which fuels curiosity, which cultivates wisdom.

THE CREATIVE HUMAN COMPUTER

The human brain is often compared to a computer, but they are actually very different. Most computers are largely information-storage devices. Ask an information-seeking question, and the computer goes into a retrieval mode—as does the human brain. However, ask an understanding-seeking question, and the mind has to make up an answer not found in the storage closet of the brain. Computers cannot make up answers. Understanding-seeking questions stimulate the kind of mental activity that creates insight or discovery. As the mind leaps and turns and twists to respond to an understanding-seeking question, special new synapses are activated and the insight experience occurs.

"Insight is the brain at play," brain researcher Pierce Howard, author of *The Owner's Manual to the Brain*, told me recently, "and the brain loves to play." Discovery—that "Aha!" experience of finding a connection, closing a gap, completing a pattern—is very rewarding to the mind. So rewarding, in fact, that the mind is constantly on the lookout for an opportunity to repeat the experience. And the more "Aha's!" the mind gets, the hungrier the mind is for them. Finding information is easy and boring; crafting information is challenging and exhilarating. The more the mind experiences creative discovery, the more the mind hunts another insight. This pursuit of insight or discovery is what we call "curiosity." To the mind, curiosity is its own reward. And the by-product of perpetual curiosity is wisdom.

HOW TO ASK QUESTIONS

How does the mentor start this insight-curiosity-wisdom chain? One major chain starter is the understanding-seeking question. Great mentors, aware that their objective is to foster wisdom, are skilled at asking these questions. Below are several important techniques for crafting and asking questions that produce insight.

Start with a setup statement

This may seem strange, but the best way to ask an insight-producing question is to start with a statement. Here's the reason: Questions can be more powerful if the sender and receiver are clearly on the same wavelength—and know that they are. Starting with a setup statement establishes identification and context. It creates a milieu that makes the follow-up question much more powerful.

Mentor: (Setup) Julie, you've been working for about eight weeks now on the Aldridge review.

To the mind, curiosity is its own reward. And the by-product of perpetual curiosity is wisdom.

Protégé: (Answer) That's right. I've had to put in some long hours on it.

Mentor: (Question) What have you learned about the project that you didn't expect to learn?

Notice how much more effective the question is after the mentor first makes a statement to establish identification (I am on your wavelength) and context (We have now established what area we are focusing on). It communicates to the protégé: I've done my homework, I care, I'm eager to learn with you. It also helps the protégé to focus cleanly on the question and not on establishing a background to shore up the answer. Imagine how defensive the question alone might make the protégé feel.

Ask questions that require higher-level thinking

Remember that the ultimate goal is to create insight, not to share information. Granted, some information sharing may be necessary; the main objective, however, is to nurture understanding and growth, not just exchange facts. Construct questions that require the protégé to dig deep to answer. Questions that force *comparisons* can accomplish this ("What are ways the Hollar project was different from the Applegate Project?"). Questions that require *synthesis* can induce deeper thinking ("What do you see as the key implications of Mr. Perdue's assessment?"). And questions that call for *evaluation* can provoke higher-level thinking ("If you could handle that assignment again, what would you do differently?").

The conventional wisdom on questioning has always been to ask open-ended questions. Closed questions, the lesson goes, will cause the receiver to deliver a short, single-word or phrase answer. However, the process is more complex than that. Socrates' understanding-seeking questions did not just make the slave talk—they made him think. Anyone with a teenager knows that the answers to questions beginning with what, how, and why can be as short as those for a yes-no

Ask an information-seeking question, you get only an answer or a fact; ask an understanding-seeking question and you unleash a more powerful chain of events.

Assessing Your Inquiry Talents

The Mentor Scale can be a helpful tool in examining your talents and blind spots with regard to inquiry. Below are a few things to watch out for, tied to the scoring form you completed in chapter 5.

Sociability

Low: *Watch out for too much silence. If the protégé does not answer in ten seconds, she may need for you to redirect the question. Also, know that eye contact can be important in conveying a sincere interest in the protégé's answers. Tape your conversations to self-evaluate your style on inquiry.*

High: *Beware of not giving the protégé an opportunity to answer. Silence can be golden. Pause after asking a question. If you are susceptible to this trap, count to ten after asking a question and before asking another or rephrasing the one you just asked. Assume that the protégé heard and understood and is simply contemplating an answer.*

Dominance

Low: *Think before you ask. You may tend to let the interaction wander by asking questions just to ask questions. Consider your goal and focus. Determine what you seek to learn, then choose questions that will take you there.*

High: *You may have a tendency to craft questions that give you the answer you like to hear. Leading the protégé is just as inappropriate and ineffective as leading the witness. Soften your tone; make sure your approach does not make the protégé feel as though she were on trial.*

Openness

Low: *Avoid keeping your questions too much on the surface. While invading privacy is not the goal, your aim is to foster in-depth thinking. Be willing to allow a bit of controversy; conflict is nothing more than a symptom of tension.*

When you accurately interpret and work through conflict by your candor and openness, interpersonal closeness and valuable creativity will be the likely by-product.

*   **High:** *You may often find yourself wanting to answer for the protégé. Back off and give the person a chance to communicate his thoughts. It is also important to avoiding getting too personal too quickly. While you may be more than ready to foster closeness, the protégé may need a bit more time.*

question. The intent of questioning to seek understanding is not just more words in the answer, but more depth in the thinking needed to produce the answer.

Avoid questions that begin with "why"

Why avoid "why" questions? In most cultures, a sentence that begins with the word "why" and ends in a question mark is usually perceived as judgmental and indicting. Granted, body language can play a role in how such questions are perceived, but even with perfect body language, our antennae go up as soon as we hear a "why" question.

Find ways to soften the interrogatory question. "Why did you do that?" can sound very different from "What were your reasons for doing that?" The word "why" is not the problem; it is putting "why" on the front of a question. As we learned earlier, judgment can turn an open atmosphere into one of protection, caution, and guarded behavior. Without vulnerability there is no risk; without risk there is no experimentation and growth.

Use curiosity to stimulate curiosity

Questions can be more powerful if the sender and receiver are clearly on the same wavelength — and know that they are.

Socrates did more than ask good questions of his slave-protégé. Socrates demonstrated an enthusiasm for the learning process. He believed in it and was excited to participate in demonstrating it. Attitude is as much a part of the Socratic method as technique.

A few years ago stereographic pictures became the rage. People stared at them for long periods, trying to find the image or object among what seemed a random mixture of colored dots. I watched a teenage girl in a shopping mall help her boyfriend "see" a picture she had earlier figured out. The girl and boy were equally curious, both eager for the image to be discovered again, both excited when the insight finally came to the boy. Mentoring is like that.

Great mentors are not only curious, they are excited by the opportunity to stimulate other people's curiosity. Their attitude is, "I can't wait to see the lights come on for you!" They are open about their excitement and verbally communicate pleasure when the protégé's "Aha!" finally comes.

Take stock of the greatest mentors down through the ages—Jesus, Buddha, Moses, Mohammed, Confucius, Lao-tse, to name a few. Their influence was due in part to their ability to challenge their learners with thought-provoking questions. The same is true of modern mentors. In a study done a few years ago, Fortune 500 CEOs were asked what contributed most to their success. Many listed an effective mentor as one of the key factors. To the question of what made these important people so influential, the most common response harked back to mead and Socrates: they asked great questions. Questions are the jewels of mentoring.

9

PUTTING THE "US" IN "TRUST"

Blending Humility and Confidence

HE MOST FAMOUS CAR in Charlotte, North Carolina, in 1971 was a perfectly restored antique Mercedes-Benz sports car owned and daily driven by Luther Hodges Jr. Luther was then chairman of the board of North Carolina National Bank and the son of a former North Carolina governor and Kennedy administration cabinet member. Tall, handsome, and Harvard educated, Luther was an impressive leader. Coupled with The Car, he was just plain impressive!

I had been with the bank only a few months and considered myself to be about 347 levels below Luther. My occasional meetings with him were always cordial, warm, and upbeat. He went out of his way to help soothe my too-obvious nervousness at being in the presence of the chairman. I wanted to learn from him—and he clearly afforded me the opportunity. However, the emotional space between us felt too wide for me. I picked my words carefully in his presence. Learning from Mr. Hodges always took a back seat to impressing Mr. Hodges. That is, until The Car changed everything.

I was accompanying Luther and my boss to a meeting in Raleigh, about three hours from Charlotte, the city where we all lived and worked. My boss and I had driven there in the company Ford checked out in his name. Luther had driven there in The Car. Our meeting ran late, so Luther and my boss decided to stay over and drive back together early the next morning so they could talk on the drive. Two small problems remained: how was I going to get back to Charlotte that evening, and how was The Car going to get back to Charlotte?

Mentoring partnerships work only when there is trust. When mentors trust protégés, protégés reciprocate in kind.

"Chip, why don't you take my car home with you?" suggested Luther, flashing his Steinway smile. "Drive into work in the morning, park in my spot, and just leave the keys with Pam. I'll give you a ride home tomorrow afternoon." My ears rang, my heart pounded, and I was unable to speak for what seemed an eternity. The *chairman* wanted me to drive The Car to *my* home! He trusted me with his most prized possession! The distance between us evaporated; suddenly I felt that Luther was my friend. My anxiety was magically transformed into confidence—and although I didn't know it at the time, that marked the beginning of my real learning.

Mentoring partnerships work only when there is trust. While trust comes from experience, the experience must involve some risk. Someone has to take a leap of faith to gain the experience to get the trust. And when mentors trust protégés, protégés reciprocate in kind.

Trust is a powerful ingredient in all healthy relationships. It makes marriages, friendships, and all manner of alliances work, and work well. However, trust has a special role in relationships in which there is an unequal distribution of power: trust is the equalizer.

PUT THE PROTÉGÉ "ON THE RIGHT"

At an early age I learned in school and church that sitting on the right was a special privilege. The Bible makes many references to "sitting at the right hand of God." Kings put their most important ally on their right when attending a banquet. Years later I learned the origin of this custom. Like people in general, most kings (and writers of Scripture) were right handed. In the era of sword and dagger, the right side was the hardest to defend for a right-handed person. To unsheathe a sword with the right hand and strike to the near right was very awkward. So the king invited the person he trusted most to sit at his most vulnerable side. It became a station of honor.

The counterpart to putting the protégé on your right is any action that deliberately, as well as symbolically, communicates trust and honor. Luther let me drive home The Car. Now that I'm on the other side of fifty, I'm a bit embarrassed to remember how I felt; it seems juvenile and immature. But if I roll my life story back twenty-five years and reflect on the experience, I remember it being the same feeling I had at age ten when my dad told me to "go get the tractor and park it in the barn."

The most effective sitting-on-the-right actions are those tailored to the individual. They dramatically demonstrate two aspects of the relationship—a deep understanding of the individual and a recognition that trust is created through trustful actions. A friend of mine remembers when his mentor sent him to an important meeting in his place. A partner describes a time when a giant in his field was unable to keep an engagement and recommended him as his replacement. A boss of

The most effective actions dramatically demonstrate two aspects of the relationship—a deep understanding of the individual and a recognition that trust is created through trustful actions.

The mentor who steps up to the plate and dramatically demonstrates humility and authenticity is the mentor who nurtures trust.

mine, unexpectedly called out of the country, asked me to interview a candidate for a very senior position in the company and offered the use of his executive-suite office for the interview. Gestures like these communicate a special trust.

DEMONSTRATE "HUMILITY SQUARED"

Johnson & Johnson, one of the most trusted organizations in the world today, enhanced their reputation during their darkest hour, the Tylenol poisoning incident. Instead of covering up the problem or making excuses, the company spent over $100 million to remove every bottle of Tylenol from shelves around the world. Though the incident was the result of sabotage, they assumed responsibility for it—and gained enormous respect and renewed trust from consumers. Actor Hugh Grant's reputation suffered only a slight blip on the screen from his escapade with a prostitute because, rather than ducking the press or denying the charges, he acknowledged his "sins" and asked for the public's forgiveness. Dee Dee Myers, former press secretary to President Clinton, fared equally well by demonstrating public humility after being stopped by police on suspicion of driving while intoxicated.

All relationships experience hiccups and less-than-perfect moments. The mentor who steps up to the plate and dramatically demonstrates humility and authenticity is the mentor who nurtures trust. Luther not only loaned me The Car, he also leveled with me about his own errors, struggles, and challenges. The more I saw of his humility, the more I trusted him.

At a large social event in Ovens Auditorium in Charlotte, North Carolina, organized to formally announce his candidacy for the U.S. Senate, Luther, relying openly and heavily on note cards, began his prepared speech. The audience listened politely. Luther was never very comfortable as a public speaker. Halfway through, he lost his place. He cracked an awkward, apologetic joke and ad-libbed for a moment as he struggled to put his cards in order. Before he could recover, the audience broke into supportive applause. It was the sincere, genuine, flawed Luther they adored, not the Luther reading his speech from notes. Mask removal is the humble stuff of which trust is made.

Humility does not require you to fall on your sword. Nor does it mean loudly advertising your warts and clay feet. It does mean working very hard to be open and vulnerable with protégés. It means remaining alert for opportunities to show empathy (I know how you feel) rather than sympathy (I feel how you feel). It means working to strip any nuance of rank, power, or status from the relationship. Mentoring is about equality, not sovereignty.

CAREFULLY COMMUNICATE COMPETENCE

Larry N. Davis and Dr. Duane Tway have broken new ground in the field of interpersonal trust. "Trust," they say, "is a state of readiness for unguarded interaction with some one or thing." We lower our human shields, they posit, only if the perceived intention of others is pure and if their perceived competence is valued. In other words, we trust those people who we believe are (1) not out to do us in, and (2) able to do what we trust them to do. We do not trust mentors to be great mentors if we believe they have little to help us learn.

The challenge in communicating competence is in not displaying arrogance at the same time. How does the mentor show smartness without being a smart aleck? While humility is always a virtue, too much can threaten the protégé's confidence in the mentor. Self-effacing comments, a symbol of modesty if used in moderation, can erode faith if carried too far. "Great leaders," said Luther

> **❝I** bid him look into the lives of men as though into a mirror, and from others to take an example for himself.❞
>
> — Terence, 190–159 BC

Hodges to one of my advanced leadership classes, "are willing to let followers see their weak sides. And they are willing to let followers see their strong sides." Call it wholeness, balance, congruence—the goal is a presence that engenders trust.

Therefore, let the protégé hear your pride in your ability. Don't boast; simply acknowledge your good fortune. Be quick to credit others where credit is due: "I was really lucky to get to understudy Tom Connellan. One of the things Tom taught me was. . . . " Indicate your eagerness to share whatever competence you possess with the protégé. Let the protégé know that although you hold something of superior value, that does not make you superior.

Trust is something that happens within people only when it is created between people.

Putting the "us" in "trust" involves remembering that trust occurs in an intimate, interpersonal dimension. Trust is something that happens *within* people only when it is created *between* people. Trust is not something that happens by accident; trust is crafted on purpose, with the mentor's full awareness of how his actions affect his protégé.

And where does this leave us with Luther and The Car? Luther lost his primary bid for the Senate seat, but went on to become undersecretary of commerce in the Carter administration, then chairman of the board of a Washington, D.C., bank. Today he manages a variety of entrepreneurial ventures all over the world from his Santa Fe office. He kept The Car for many years, finally selling it in D.C. After twenty-five years, we still correspond. And there are very few people in the world I trust more than Chairman Hodges.

P A R T

III

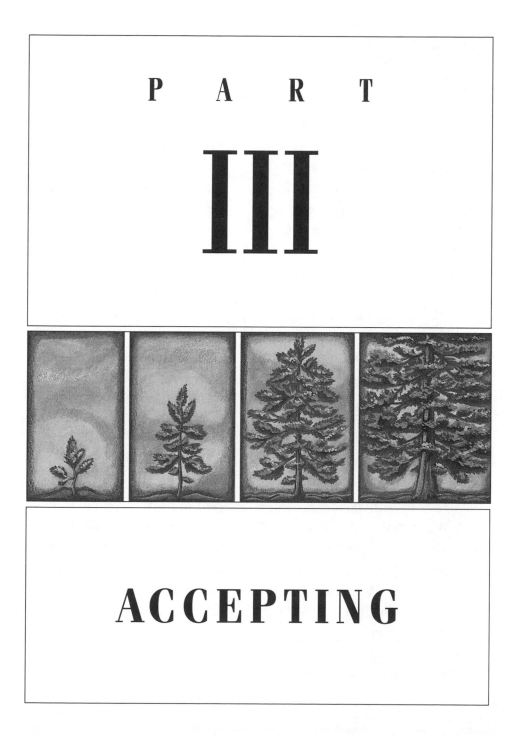

ACCEPTING

Pope John XXIII was probably the most beloved pope of this century. The devotion people felt for him was due in part to the fact that he was completely without pretense. His openness and humility endeared him to millions, Catholic and non-Catholic alike. One of his first official acts was to visit the prisoners in a large penal institution in Rome. As he gave the inmates his blessing, he shared with them the fact that he had been in a prison, too—to visit his cousin!

Sidney Jourard, in his classic The Transparent Self, *describes countless research studies demonstrating conclusively that humans have a natural, built-in tendency to be open and revealing. When that tendency is thwarted, the individual reacts by becoming closed, cautious, and reserved. The longer this blockage occurs, the more difficult it is for trusting relationships to develop. In* Why Am I Afraid to Tell You Who I Am?, *John Powell answers the title question of his book, "Because if I tell you who I am, you may not like who I am, and it's all that I have."*

In the last few chapters we explored different dimensions of the core competency surrendering. *In part III we will examine the second crucial core competency of great mentoring:* accepting. *Mentors effective at demonstrating acceptance have a powerful impact on the mentoring process. Accepting is evaluation-free, egalitarian encountering— mentoring without arrogance, bias, prejudice, or selectivity.*

Mentors show acceptance in several ways. One of these could be called "mask removal"—the willingness to be open and vulnerable. We all wear masks, in part to protect ourselves against rejection. When a mentor removes this mask in front of the protégé, it changes the nature of the relationship from cautious to unguarded. Energy normally devoted to cover and protection becomes available for insight and discovery.

Accepting mentors avoid testing tones, a disapproving countenance, and parental gestures like pointing fingers and hands on hips. They seek to foster a spirit of inquiry on a level emotional playing field—a relationship with unrestricted access, from which all issues unrelated to learning are barred.

Accepting means that you are being assertively honest and candid, with the intention of helping, not hurting, the other person. There is a cleanness

and frankness about relationships in which acceptance is valued. Great mentors care enough to be honest and forthright; they are also curious and learning oriented enough to invite and accept candor from the protégé.

The following four chapters focus on skills and techniques that support the accepting competence. This part begins with the most crucial accepting skill, dramatic listening, and ends with the most challenging, managing learner resistance.

10

EAR OF AN ALLY

The Lost Art of Listening

I'LL BET there are not more than two supervisors on the face of the globe who do not sense the importance of being a good listener! It matters not whether the person has ever attended a leadership class, read an article on supervision, or studied a manager who is a good listener. If you've never heard of the importance of listening, you're a card-carrying alien from some other galaxy!

Knowing that listening is important and *being* a good listener are two very different things. Ask employees about the listening skills of their bosses, and most will give them at best a C-plus. With zillions of books on how leaders should listen, why do employees continue to ding their bosses on listening? Is this a competence crisis?

In my experience, the gap between "should" and "would" has less to do with communication management than with noise management. Most leaders *can* be great listeners. Let their eight-year-old come home crying about a neighborhood conflict and you will see great listening. Zero in on a quiet corner conversation in the funeral home during the wake for a friend and you will see great listening. Put a leader between a hostile union steward and potential shut-you-down strike and you will witness some of the best listening in history. Yet, mix the normal pace of work, the typical persona of "I'm the boss," and the traditional orientation that "employees don't need to be babied," and you have the prescription for "just get to the punch line" leader listening.

> **66***H*e holds him with his glittering eye—
> The wedding guest stood still,
> And listens like a three year's child:
> The Mariner hath his will.***99**
>
> — Samuel T. Coleridge

Listening is crucial to mentoring. Ask fifty people who had great mentors what attribute they found most crucial, and forty-nine will probably mention their mentors' listening: "I felt I had his undivided attention when I most needed it." "You felt there was absolutely nothing happening on the face of the globe but you, her, and your problem." "He was so engaged in my concern that his secretary had to interrupt us to tell him his phone had been ringing. *I* sure wasn't going to mention it."

How do the best mentors evade the demands of daily distractions to give dedicated listening? The sounds of great listening tell us effective listeners don't *start* doing anything special—they *stop* doing something normal.

FOCUS ON FOCUS

Great mentors get focused and stay focused. When listening is their goal, they make it *the* priority. They do not let *anything* distract. A wise leader once said, "There are no individuals at work more important to your success than your employees—not your boss, not your customers, not your vendors." When an employee needs you to listen, pretend you just got a gift of five minutes with your greatest hero. For me, it's Abraham Lincoln. What a great concept! Think about it. If you could have five minutes—and *only* five minutes—with Moses, Mozart, or Margaret Mead, would you let a call from your boss, your customer, or *anyone* eat up part of that precious time? Treat your employees with the same focus and priority.

"Hold my calls," "Let's get out of here so we can really talk," or "Tell him I'll have to call back" are words that telegraph noise management. They say to employees, "What you have to say is so important that I don't want to miss a single word." If you cannot give employees the "I've got five minutes with Kissinger" kind of focus, postpone the encounter until you can. It's better to say, "Jane, I want to give you my undivided attention. But I'm two hours from a crucial meeting and, to be perfectly honest, I would be giving you only half of my attention. Can we schedule this later today when I can really focus?"

ASSUME THE REPORTER POSITION

Try this the next time you need to listen to someone: Imagine that you're a newspaper reporter from another culture, sent here on assignment to get the story and report it. Your readers cannot see, hear, or feel this story except through your words. They also know nothing about the culture; you must rely on every tiny clue, nuance, and symbol to get the story right.

Your first interviewee is sitting before you, talking. It is your protégé. Now, in your role as a foreign reporter, describe every subtlety in the protégé's tone, gesture, or expression.

If you could have five minutes—and only five minutes—with Moses, Mozart, or Margaret Mead, would you let a call from your boss, your customer, or anyone eat up part of that precious time?

Notice especially the eyes—what some have called the "windows to the soul." Pretend you do not know this person and are hearing her speak to you for the first time. Listen for her choice of words and expressions. Is there a deeper meaning behind the sentences you hear? Is there a message that is not initially obvious in the communication?

Dramatic listening is not just a rendezvous of brains; it is a uniting, a linkage, a partnership. Like all human connections, it requires constant effort and commitment.

If you ask a question or make a statement, how quick is the protégé's response? What might be implied by her silence? Is her laughter polite, muted, or hearty? If her words and tone could be a song, what style of music would it be—a country song, a rap tune, a chorale, a gospel hymn? If a great painter were to use this person's words as the inspiration for a picture, what might appear on the canvas? What color is the protégé's tone or mood?

Listening, done well, is complete absorption. Ever watch Larry King on CNN? His success as an interviewer lies not in his questions but in his terrific listening skills. He zips right past the interviewee's words, sentences, and paragraphs to get to the meaning. The mission of listening is to be so tuned into the other person's message that understanding becomes a copy-and-paste function from one mind to another. Perhaps the expression "meeting of the minds" should be changed to "joining of the minds." Dramatic listening is not just a rendezvous of brains; it is a uniting, a linkage, a partnership. Like all human connections, it requires constant effort and commitment.

BE A MIRROR, NOT A MEMORY

One of my biggest challenges in striving to be a good parent was simply to listen without an agenda. Whenever my son began to catalog his concerns, convictions, or curiosity, I would usually feel the need to make a point, teach a lesson, correct an action, or offer some caution. When I finally gave up trying to be a smart daddy and worked at being simply a mirror, he began to open up, trust, and—most importantly—feel heard.

When he asked, "How would you . . . ?" before I offered an opinion I would work hard to remember to ask what he would do. When he voiced frustration or concern, before I answered I tried first to communicate through my actions that his message had gotten through—especially when my answer was likely to be different from the one he thought he was going to get. The ancient adage "You are not eligible to change my view until you first show that you understand my view" serves you in two ways. First, it helps you stay focused on being heard rather than making points. Second, it tells your listener that he is important.

PUT YOUR PROTÉGÉ IN CHARGE OF CUEING YOU

Being a poor listener is habit forming. Focusing takes effort; mirroring takes patience. Meanwhile, the clock is ticking on getting that order out, the boss wants to know where's the Anderson report you promised to have done yesterday, two calls are on hold, three people are pacing the waiting room, and you're finishing up a meeting with your protégé. Who could be a great listener under these circumstances? Answer: Not even Superman! You need assistance from the only person who can help you—your protégé!

Focusing takes effort; mirroring takes patience.

Here's how you ask for it: "Kristin, I need your help. I know there are times when I'm not the listener I want to be. But most of the time when I'm being a lousy listener, I'm not aware I'm doing it. That's where you can help. When you think you're not getting my undivided attention, I'd appreciate your letting me know. I may get better, I may reschedule our meeting to a better time, or I may just keep on being a lousy listener. But I don't have a shot at improving unless I know when I need to, and you're the best person to tell me."

Protégés are not stupid. They will hear the words of your request, but they'll be skeptical until they see you act. You may have to ask several times before your protégé takes you at your

Ask fifty people who had great mentors what attribute they found most crucial, and forty-nine will probably mention their mentors' listening.

word. And unless you express your gratitude—no matter how accurate the assessment or how successful the result—your protégé may decide not to risk your displeasure, and withdraw. Prime the feedback pump, conscientiously listen to and value whatever you get, and, in time, the quality and helpfulness of the feedback will improve.

Good mentors do not listen passively; they listen dramatically. They demonstrate through their words and actions that the thoughts of their protégés are welcome and useful. When people feel heard, they feel valued. Feeling valued, they are more likely to take risks and experiment. Only through trying new steps do they grow and learn. The bottom line is this: If your goal is to be a great mentor, start by using your noise-management skills to help you fully use your talents as a great listener.

11

"GIVE-AND-TAKE" STARTS WITH "GIVE"

Distinguished Dialogues

D IALOGUE IS DEFINED as an "interchange of ideas, especially when open and frank, as in seeking mutual understanding or harmony." Effective dialogue—with emphasis on "di," meaning "two"—requires a level playing field, equality, and give-and-take. These dynamics raise dialogue from a simple

> **"R**eal isn't how you are made,"
> said the Skin Horse. "It's a thing
> that happens to you. . . . It doesn't
> happen all at once, you become. It
> takes a long time. That's why it
> doesn't often happen to people who
> break easily, or have sharp edges, or
> who have to be carefully kept.**"**
>
> —Margery Williams, *The Velveteen Rabbit*

question-and-answer session to a rich, creative interaction that is more than the sum of its parts.

Recall the conversations you most valued. What elements made the dialogue positive and productive? You can probably identify several. First, each player valued the viewpoint of the other, even if the views were different. The give-and-take was one in which both parties could give undivided attention and keep the dialogue focused. Finally, the outcome was that learning occurred, issues were resolved, or understanding was reached. These three components—valuing, give-and-take, and closure—will form the basis of our look at dialogue in the mentoring relationship.

THE MAGIC OF MIND SET

There is a moment in the Edward Albee play *Who's Afraid of Virginia Woolf?* in which George and Martha (played in the film version by Richard Burton and Elizabeth Taylor) stop their perpetual verbal battle to discover that they have been arguing over completely different subjects. The same thing often happens, at various decibel levels, in our own conversations. "What were we talking about?" "I forgot what I was saying," "Where were we?" tell us that we're involved in off-track, out-of-sync, or unrelated conversations.

"Mind set" is the term for the tone-setting actions at the beginning of a discussion that ensure a meeting of the minds on three simple but powerful questions. If both mentor and protégé are of one mind on these questions, the discussion will probably have a positive outcome.

Why are we here?

Both parties need to be clear on the purpose of the conversation. A simple statement followed by confirmation is usually enough: "Rachel, I see this session as an opportunity for the two of us to discuss the best approach for conducting the Boyd study. Is that your goal as well?"

What will it mean to you?

The potential for both participants to benefit from the dialogue is important. Not only does it help focus the exchange, it enhances motivation. Proper attention to the potential benefits for the protégé can turn a lethargic, "Here we go again, another meeting with Gilbert" mind set into "Wow, this meeting with Gilbert is going to be really helpful!" The mentor derives the satisfaction of helping the protégé learn to the benefit of all.

How shall we talk?

Mind set also includes telegraphing the tone and style needed. Even if the tone is implied, a brief reminder can be useful in serving notice that an open, candid, freewheeling conversation is needed and expected. It also helps clarify the rules of engagement, avoiding unpleasant surprises. "Mary Nell, I'll be as open and candid as I can in this discussion. My thought was that we devote about thirty minutes to exploring options, then give you a chance to make a decision."

PRIMING THE PUMP

The expression "priming the pump" had real meaning when I was a child. In the backyard of my grandfather's home was a water pump that required priming to function. You "seeded" water from the ground by pouring a large pitcher of water into the top and then pumping madly up and down on the handle. To a young boy who thought that water came from a faucet, "water making"—wringing water out of the earth by your own efforts—had special magic.

If there is ever a time when the word "catalyst" applies to the role of mentor, it is during dialogue.

If there is ever a time when the word "catalyst" applies to the role of mentor, it is during dialogue. The human version of priming the pump is assisting insight making by helping the discussion accomplish its function. There are five skills associated with catalyzing the give-and-take of dialogue: asking initiating or clarifying questions, paraphrasing, summarizing, extending, and using nonverbal cues.

Ask initiating and clarifying questions

An earlier chapter on Socrates' secret (chapter 8) explored the art of stimulating learning by asking questions. The questions that work best are those that are direct but not leading— especially open-ended questions, those beginning with what, when, where, or how. Here are some examples of open-ended questions helpful in initiating and clarifying:

- ► "What was the most challenging part of the task?"

- ► "How did your team approach the problem?"

- ► "Describe what makes this technique important."

- ► "What are your remaining questions?"

- ► "What have I not asked that you think would be helpful for me to know?"

Paraphrase

The purpose of paraphrasing is to demonstrate that you are listening and that you understand what is being communicated— as though holding a mirror to the discussion. Protégés appreciate knowing that they have been heard accurately, and this serves to prime the discussion pump.

There are four types of paraphrasing:

1. **Restatement.** In your own words, rather than the protégé's, state a condensed version of what the protégé said. Don't simply parrot or repeat the protégé's exact

words; this communicates that you heard the protégé's statement, but not that you understood it.

2. **General to specific.** If the protégé's statement is a generalization, you might paraphrase it in more specific terms by expanding on one part of the statement or by giving an example. By stating the specific, you show that you understand the general.

3. **Specific to general.** If the protégé's statement is specific, paraphrase by stating a generalization or principle. By formulating a broader response, you indicate not only that you understand the protégé's statement, but also that the protégé's statement can, in fact, be generalized.

4. **Restatement in opposite terms.** Convey that you understand the meaning of the protégé's statement by restating it in opposite terms. For example, if the protégé says that a manager should do something, you can restate by saying that the manager should not do the opposite.

Consider the following statement: "Effective auditing requires the auditor to have a special kind of cautious optimism." As mentor, you might paraphrase this statement in any of the following ways:

► **Restatement:** "You are saying that the auditor should be open but still careful."

► **General to specific:** "An auditor should carefully check every entry."

► **Specific to general:** "Sounds as though you think auditing is complex."

► **Restatement in opposite terms:** "You mean that the auditor should not be negative and overly suspicious."

The goal of paraphrasing is not to ask a question or make an exclamation. Make certain your inflection turns down, not up.

Paraphrasing encourages protégés to say more because they know they have been understood. An important point to remember is to look for a sign that the protégé agrees with your interpretation. If no sign is given, either verbal or nonverbal, ask the protégé whether you've paraphrased the statement accurately. If you make mistakes without checking, then you are demonstrating misunderstanding, which will fog the discussion and dampen the learning climate.

One last point on paraphrasing: Notice in the examples above that each sentence ends in a period. The goal of paraphrasing is to mirror or reflect your understanding, not to ask a question or make an exclamation. Make certain your inflection turns down, not up.

Summarize

Summarizing is similar to paraphrasing. The difference is that the goal of paraphrasing is to *mirror the meaning* to check for understanding, whereas the goal of summarizing is to *synthesize* to check for understanding. You synthesize by condensing the meaning of the protégé's comments into a sentence or two (or, if the comments were lengthy, into a paragraph) and repeating the synthesized information as a summary.

Summarizing typically begins with such phrases as

▶ "In other words . . ."

▶ "What you're saying is that . . .", and

▶ "In summary, you think that . . ."

Be careful about how you use certain phrases when summarizing. For example, too many uses of a catch phrase such as "What I hear you saying is . . ." can begin to sound mechanical and condescending.

Extend

The purpose of extending is to add scope or depth to a protégé's comments. If what you add matches the spirit of what the protégé said, it not only communicates understanding but also enriches or expands understanding. Either technical information or information about personal views and feelings can be extended.

Technical information refers to building on the factual content of the protégé's comment. An example might be, "You make a good point about the auditor's role in analyzing the corporation's financial statement. In addition, the auditor needs to ensure that all current regulations are met."

Information about personal views and feelings is what a learner says about herself during the discussion. You can add to this kind of information, but do so with care. It is a very powerful method for demonstrating deep understanding, but it is also quite difficult to do convincingly and effectively. Extending in this way requires you to empathize strongly with the protégé. Here are two examples of what a mentor might say when extending personal information:

"So you advised your colleague to sue. I was once in exactly the same position. I supervised the EEO function of human resources, and. . . ."

"I agree. After I recovered from the initial shock of my father's Alzheimer's disease, I felt lonely and angry as well."

Use gestures and body stance

Your nonverbal behavior can prime the pump of discussion and contribute to a positive learning environment by helping to communicate your understanding. Conversely, certain nonverbal behaviors can have a detrimental effect: shaking your head in disapproval, rolling your eyes to the ceiling, frowning, or suddenly moving forward in your chair. These may convey a negative judgment and make the protégé less inclined to take risks.

An appropriate gesture is to nod your head or say "uh-huh" to indicate understanding and encourage further dialogue. But don't overdo either of these cues or the protégé may feel that you are trying to manipulate the discussion rather than simply listening and encouraging.

Nonverbal cues can prime the pump and help communicate your understanding.

Jack Gamble on Dialogues
("Mentoring in Action" Revisited)

Jack took another stab at the issue. "How does he react when you get stern and serious?"

"I'm not sure," Tracy responded.

Jack tried again. "Let me ask it this way: If I asked Adam to candidly describe you when the two of you talk about his performance, what words would he use?"

Tracy's demeanor began to change. It was as if the wheels of wisdom were turning in her head.

"He would say I was relentlessly patient." She was still half lost in thought. "What else?"

Tracy responded with near excitement in her voice. "He would not describe me as tough, demanding, or disciplined."

Jack sensed that she was solving her own issue. Again, he paused before raising another question. He knew instinctively that pace was everything when insight was the goal. "So, what do you think should be your next step?"

Tracy began to outline steps: a serious conversation, a performance plan, short-term goals with clear feedback, supervision with a shorter leash, and, above all, less understanding and more discipline. Jack offered a few ideas, but mostly affirmation and encouragement. They parted with an agreement to revisit the issue in a few days.

MAINTAINING AUTHENTICITY

A discussion of discussions would be incomplete without addressing the issue of authenticity. When using any of the techniques described in this chapter, it is vital that you be authentic rather than artificial or manipulative. Discussions are opportunities for protégés to enhance their learning, not for the mentor to teach. Stay out of the way as much as possible to let the protégé do her own thinking. Try not to dominate the discussion. You need not comment on everything the protégé says. Sometimes a simple "Good!" or "Thank you" is best.

I was team teaching a service leadership class for a utility's senior management group with Glenn Kiser, a Charlotte-based consultant and gifted mentor of leaders and high-performance teams. Mostly engineers, the people in the group were struggling to make the concept of authenticity a logical part of their leadership qualities. If a concept lacks a formula, a rational explanation, or some dissectable characteristic, some engineers tend to toss it on the pile of "touchy-feely" ideas not to be taken seriously.

"So what *is* authenticity?" asked one of the more skeptical participants. My mind raced through images of velveteen rabbits, analogies of mask removal, and stories of great leaders willing to be jarringly genuine.

Glenn read my pause, sensed my struggle, and rescued me with a show-stopping question of the skeptic: "Did your daughter come visit you on Take Your Daughter to Work Day?"

The executive answered as Glenn thought he would: "Yeah, but what's your point?"

Glenn waited until the classroom fell silent. "The 'you' that you were when your daughter was watching you is what authenticity looks like."

"Oh," said the executive, suddenly humbled—and guilt-stricken—by the memory.

Authenticity and humility are powerful components of all successful learning organizations. One effective executive begins most major staff meetings by having each participant complete this sentence: "One thing I screwed up on this week was . . . , and what I learned from it was . . . ." The executive typically begins the self-revelation and sometimes gently goads participants if their "screw ups" reflect minimum risk taking. The practice not only encourages appropriate risk taking, the authenticity fosters a judgment-free setting for learning to be nurtured.

DOS AND DON'TS FOR DIALOGUES

Dialogues are interpersonal crucibles for blending facts, figures, and feelings to concoct acumen and understanding. Dialogues are most powerful when you

- ▶ listen.

- ▶ do not teach.

- ▶ allow disagreement.

- ▶ create a warm, encouraging climate.

- ▶ are aware of the learning that is taking place.

- ▶ work as hard to learn from them as you hope they do from you.

- ▶ do not pressure protégés to answer or behave as you think they should.

SCARED STUDENTS

When Fear and Learning Collide

EAR HAS A LONG and checkered career as an educational tool. Ask a high-school counselor and an army drill sergeant about the role of fear in learning and you will get two entirely different answers. In the movie *Stand and Deliver,* Edward James Olmos demonstrates a mentoring style completely at odds with John Houseman's in *The Paper Chase.* (Both films were based on real

people. Houseman played Professor Kingsfield, a fictional character based on a real law-school professor. Olmos portrayed Jaime Escalante, a true-life hero of education in Los Angeles.) Some say fear is a healthy partner with learning where simple motor skills are involved—boot camps, skydiving schools, police academies. However, most law students would not consider their intimidating law-school experience as learning a subject that was simple or motor. The debate continues.

This chapter is built on the premise that fear is far more a liability than an asset where learning is involved. A testing, contentious learning environment may bring out the adrenaline but does not bolster aptitude. Learners who are fearful tend to take fewer risks. A work environment that is continually evaluative may discourage growth by minimizing the trial-and-error behavior needed for effective learning.

Nevertheless, some work settings deliberately and consciously infuse evaluation into the setting. A major accounting firm cultivates an up-or-out philosophy, pushing young professionals to make partner by their late thirties or stand ready to be "made available to the industry." A certain well-known computer software company demonstrates a low tolerance for error by telling new recruits, "The cream rises to the top," "If you can't stand the heat, get out of the kitchen," or "At Bitbucket, Inc., only the strong survive." Likewise, one large manufacturing company anchors its inspection style on a "Do it right the first time" philosophy. Since the mentor may have little or no control over the evaluative work environment, how does mentoring work best when the protégé is scared?

> **"*Education is the ability to listen to almost anything without losing your temper or your self-confidence.*"**
>
> — Robert Frost

The factors in fear reduction are cut from the same philosophical cloth as establishing rapport (see chapter 6). However, the approach is different in that "create" is replaced with "overcome." While the focus in creating rapport is one of support and openness, the focus in overcoming fear is on strength and compassion. The emphasis is more on weaning than on welcoming.

IRRATIONAL FEELINGS ARE STILL LEGITIMATE FEELINGS

My father passed away in late 1995 at eighty-four, having suffered for his last few years from dementia—an Alzheimer's-like condition that caused his once-sharp mind slowly to deteriorate. Needless to say, to watch this former teacher-coach-banker-farmer go from superintelligent to sadly incoherent was a painful experience for the entire family. Five weeks before he died, my wife, Nancy, and I visited him. His encounter with her gave me new insight into communicating with fear.

One evening Nancy sat beside him and began to talk with him as if he were normal. He responded by pointing in the air and saying, "There! They're coming to take my land!" She pointed to the same spot and asked, "Are they there?" "Yes," he replied, "and they're mad at me!" She again focused her attention on the imaginary villains and quietly asked, "Might they be coming to visit you because they're worried about you?" There was silence for one or two minutes; then my father smiled and said, "I think you might be onto something." His fear waning, he moved to a new level of mental awareness, and for a time he conversed with her almost as he had years earlier.

Granted, there *are* rational fears. In a foxhole, the fear of being killed is rational. In a fire, the fear of getting burned is rational. At the dentist, the fear of discomfort and pain is rational. There are also rational going-to-work fears. Most fears, however, are not logical—they are psychological. That means they are as imaginary as the villains in the air were to my dad. They are also just as real!

The important contribution the mentor can make in a learning situation is to treat all fears as rational. To say to

A work environment that is continually evaluative may discourage growth by minimizing the trial-and-error behavior needed for effective learning.

someone who feels scared, "You should not feel that way," is discounting, devaluing, and discourteous. Recall the old adage, "It's easier to turn a mule if you first get him moving." To overcome fear, start where the protégé is, accepting that position as legitimate. My wife started where my dad was—and from there was able to work with him to bring him out of the grip of his fear.

FEAR IS A THREATENED NEED

Occasions for physical fear are rare in organizational life. Most employees don't worry about getting cement shoes or letter bombs. Physical violence occurs mostly in the funny pages (see Dagwood's tribulations in "Blondie"). On the contrary, organizational fears are generally psychological. People worry about getting rejected, looking foolish, losing power, appearing incompetent, being unemployed—a wide range of fears short of getting booted through a window by Mr. Dithers.

It is not the role of the mentor to become a shrink and psychoanalyze the protégé. However, to be effective in reducing fear, the mentor needs a clear understanding of the protégé's emotional state. If the stated fear is "I'm not getting a fair shot at the Melissa Bryant position," what is the real fear? If you can zero in on the real fear, or answer the stated fear while addressing the real fear, your counsel will be more effective.

Organizational fears are generally psychological. People worry about getting rejected, looking foolish, losing power, appearing incompetent, being unemployed.

Psychological needs or drives are the major energy source for individual actions; fear is a secondary response. Think of it as the flip side of a high-priority psychological need. For purposes of this book, let's assume that everyone you mentor places highest value on one of four needs—achievement, recognition, power, or control.

Getting a finer bead on the protégé's priority need is a fundamental part of effective mentoring. As you observe the protégé's actions, keep in mind these four basic needs. You will find them revealing. (Before we go any further, it is important to say that humans are far too complex to be boxed into just one of four categories. We all have these needs; we differ in part based on the priority that particular needs play in our lives. My high need for control might not be that big a deal in your life; your high need for achievement might be a low priority for me. Both of us have needs for control and achievement; we differ in the relative importance they have in our scheme of things.)

Need for achievement. People who give achievement a high priority are driven in part by a need to measure up, to do well, to succeed. They value challenge and closure and require freedom to perform. They are frustrated by barriers to opportunity. They value performance feedback ("This is very creative work") over personal feedback ("You are a very creative person"). They enjoy the professional respect of others but generally do not waste energy being concerned about what others think of them. Their offices tend to be furnished with items that are practical and that assist them in achieving a goal.

Need for recognition. Many people are driven by a need for affirmation, respect, and the adoration of others. They engage in actions that gain them approval. They tend to avoid interpersonal conflict, fearing rejection. They value personal feedback, particularly from people in authority. They enjoy being popular with others and are typically (but not universally) highly social. They often display articles that communicate relationships, such as family or group photos, or items that invite the observer to make an affirming comment.

Need for power. People with power as a high-priority need enjoy dominance over others. They demand respect and loyalty. They can be temperamental and explosive, especially on issues of loyalty or the potential of losing dominance. They can be passive or aggressive bullies, surrounding themselves with people they can dominate. They put energy into symbols of power and status as confirmation to themselves and reminders to others. Whether title, club, car, or corner office, they require signs of authority.

The important contribution the mentor can make in a learning situation is to treat all fears as rational.

Need for control. The need to control has behavioral similarities with the need for power. However, the focus is less on domination of people and more on domination of events or situations. Control people tend to be nitpickers, often devoting energy to form over substance. If their control is threatened, they quickly become frustrated, sometimes resorting to fits and pouts. They are generally on top of the details of their operation, even though their need for order might show up as an obsession with neatness.

So—what to do with all of this? Several steps can transform your observations into better understanding of your protégé. Pay close attention to her actions and ask: What need might she be fulfilling by selecting this action? Examine moments of anger. Anger, like fear, is a secondary feeling; the root issue is generally a frustrated need. People with a high need for achievement have a fear of failing; people with a high need for affirmation have a fear of rejection; people with a high need for power have a fear of appearing weak; and people with a high need for control have a fear of being wrong. Paying close attention to moments of anger can give you helpful insights into the protégé's priority needs. Remember, the higher priority the need plays in the protégé's life, the more fearful (and angry) she will be if she feels a threat to her need.

Look at the possessions the protégé chooses and displays. If you see awards or degrees on the wall, what does that tell you about the person? What about someone who displays pictures of family or friends? What kind of person drives a flashy sports car? Any one of these factors by itself may tell you little. However, an accumulation of observations, the overall pattern of behavior, can give you vital insights into the things that are most important to the protégé.

Let's assume you now have a clearer understanding of the person. What's next? Remember my earlier advice? Answer the literal words of a question while you address the deeper issue that you think might be fueling the protégé's fear.

FEAR IS A MIRROR OF SELF-ESTEEM

Last year I experienced a bit of nostalgia overload. I sent copies of my last book, *Customers As Partners,* to the sixty-two members of my high-school graduating class. Since I had not been able to attend my twentieth- or thirtieth-year class reunions, it was a chance to make some personal contact. Besides, the book contained many references to high-school stories we had all shared. The letters I received from a number of classmates were very telling. Some of the "least likely to succeed" had done extremely well in the ways society traditionally defines success. And some of the most promising had not done as well as expected.

As I read their "Let me tell you about the last thirty years" stories, I began to see a link between fear and self-esteem. As some of the "least likelies" gained confidence after high school, they discovered skills and abilities they had been unaware of in high school, and they rose to new heights, gaining self-confidence. And as Mister and Miss Senior-High Popularity came face to face with the real world outside Telfair County High School, a world in which they were no longer "cool," they began to learn about insecurity, and their lives stayed stuck in the early '60s.

Mentors can play a major role in bolstering the protégé's low self-esteem and thus pushing fear out. Mentors do not *give* courage, they *uncover* courage. Their actions help the protégé find hidden courage through actions like the following:

Think of fear as the flip side of a high-priority psychological need.

Use lots of positive affirmations! Mentors sometimes approach protégés as though affirmations were rare and expensive gifts to be doled out parsimoniously. Somewhere they heard that too much praise would make a protégé lazy. This is a sad fallacy. William James, the great psychologist-philosopher, said it well: "The deepest craving of humans is the need to be appreciated." Look for things to compliment; lavish praise with sincerity and enthusiasm.

Assume that the protégé has no reason for low self-esteem.
This means never buying the legitimacy of a protégé's low opinion of himself. While this may sound harsh, it can be a powerful gift. This subtle message in the mentor's attitude will
become self-fulfilling and in time help the protégé let go of the
old self-view and assume a new feeling of worth. Remember *My
Fair Lady*? Professor Henry Higgins wanted to see if he could
take a lowly flower girl from the streets of London and train her
so well that he could pass her off as a member of the nobility
at an upper-crust ball. As Eliza Doolittle learned the ways and
speech of an aristocratic lady, she became one.

Fear is a barrier to learning. When protégés bring fear into a
learning environment, they limit the depth and breadth of their
growth. Great mentors are fear hunters. Invite your protégé to
hunt fear with you, and together you will enjoy the bounty of
your success.

TRADING POWER FOR RESPECT

When Pupils Are Peers

HEN MY son was a fourth-grader, he came home one day and announced that he had a new teacher assistant.

"Did your old teacher assistant leave?" I asked. "No," he replied, "Mrs. Greer is still there."

"What's your new teacher assistant's name?" I asked. Without looking up from kicking his soccer ball, he responded matter-of-factly: "Tommy."

I instantly knew this was weird. Fourth-graders don't refer to their teachers by their first names. Tenth-graders use teachers' first names as an act of rebellion; twelfth-graders do it to sound grown up and cool. But most fourth-graders are not interested in being rebellious or cool.

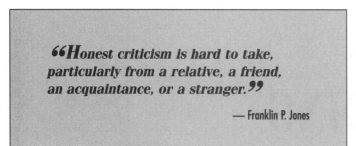

"Honest criticism is hard to take, particularly from a relative, a friend, an acquaintance, or a stranger."

— Franklin P. Jones

As it turned out, Tommy was a sixth-grader and a part of a cross-age education effort to let older students tutor younger students. The concept was that elementary students often respond better to older peers than to a teacher, and placing teaching responsibility on the older students increased their growth as well.

Four months into my son's experience, I asked how he and Tommy were doing. "He's not a helper any more," he replied. I decided to keep my mouth closed to see if he would fill me in. He continued, "Tommy thought he knew more about math than me. And when I started getting answers faster than he did, he got really mad. He started calling me names. Mrs. Greer heard him and took his job away from him."

Peer mentoring has always had special challenges. Resistance, always an obstacle in mentoring, is especially acute when the mentor and protégé are peers. Most peer-mentors are painfully aware of how labels like "smart aleck" and "know-it-all" stick to those who profess to have wisdom they want to share. How do you make peer mentoring work when resistance so easily raises its ugly head?

HUMILITY FIRST

Humility is a special gift of managers who succeed as mentors. It is more than a gift for peer mentoring—it's the key to the front door. If you start off with peers by showing off your expertise, you're guaranteed to lose your non-captive audience. With bosses, you *have* to listen, and perhaps even *act* interested—but peers will simply blow you off and not waste their time.

Humility is not a synonym for apology. Humble means unassuming and egoless, acting from the soul without adding anything. You can be both humble and confident.

ASK LOTS OF QUESTIONS UP FRONT

Most protégés, when confronted with a mentor who is also a peer, show resistance at first: "What the heck could you teach me?" "Who appointed you Mister Know-It-All?" Just like mentors, protégés sometimes harbor the notion that mentors should be superior. Any deviation from the traditional order of things makes them nervous. It is therefore critical that the peer-mentor allay protégé anxieties and deal with the resistance.

One way to deal with resistance is to put enormous focus, energy, and attention on the protégé early in the relationship. Demonstrate dramatic listening. Forget about reciprocity for a while. Let the interest be one-sided—yours in the protégé. You'll get your turn later. Think of it this way: Every time you ask a question of the protégé, you gain a point. Every time you make a statement, you lose a point. And every time you make a statement about your background, your interest, your experience, or your anything, you lose five points. Get as many points as you can in the first ten minutes of the encounter.

When you meet resistance with resistance, growth comes to a screeching halt.

AVOID CONDITIONAL AFFIRMATIONS

My first job fresh out of college was as a management trainee in a large New Mexico bank. I started my one-year rotational training program as a teller in a small branch. After mastering the complexities of being a paying and receiving teller in a little over a month, I became the teller who balanced first at the

Gauging Peer Mentoring

The Mentor Scale can serve as an early warning device on peer mentoring. Take a quick review of your profile in chapter 5. If you've had a recent experience mentoring a peer, take a few minutes and recall the highs, lows, joys, and sorrows. Remember the times you felt the mentoring relationship was not working as well as it could. What was happening? Recall the times the relationship seemed to go very well. Now scan the cautions below as you plan for your next peer-mentoring experience.

Sociability

Low: Did you see the whole experience as more chore than glee? Did you find your mind wandering, preoccupied with all the other tasks you could be doing? If you elect to do peer mentoring, be prepared to give it more intense energy and greater passion than you are accustomed to giving. It will serve you well by elevating the relationship to a level that will reward you with what you get back.

High: Did you find your peer sometimes wanting to end the meeting before it seemed time? Did your sessions sometimes wander off into areas unrelated to your purpose or focus? Were some meetings more about laughing than learning? You endanger the relationship when you allow the social side to severely overshadow the purposeful-growth side. Look for other contexts or settings to visit. Let your mentoring encounters be remembered as highly focused and productive.

Dominance

Low: Did your peer-protégé ever ask you, "What are we supposed to be doing?" "Why are we meeting?" or "Are we going to have to meet again on this?" Mentoring takes leadership and purposeful energy. Leadership does not have to be high-control supervision, but you do need clear, focused energy to move toward a goal. Let your peer-protégé see your conviction and commitment through your dynamism.

High: Did you find yourself involved in too many arguments? Did your peer-protégé often disagree with your position? Or did you get no push-back when you might normally have expected a debate? In future peer-mentoring situations, allow your protégé to share in the leadership. Let your protégé hear you deliver more questions than answers. Precede "Here's what I think" with "What do you think?"

Openness

Low: Did you sense that your peer-protégé was holding something back? Did you find yourself having to work hard to get your peer-protégé to level with you? Did the relationship have a reserve or cautiousness about it? Be willing in your next peer-mentoring experience to express more of your feelings than you might be comfortable with. Describe an experience in which you made a mistake. Get out of your head; let yourself say not just "I think," but "I feel."

High: Did your peer-protégé seem tense or uncomfortable? If you had taken a movie of your mentoring sessions, would it show that you were clearly leading the relationship pretty much throughout? Was there considerably more energy and passion coming from you than from your protégé? Remember, vulnerability is a positive quality, but it needs to be nurtured to come forth, not jerked out. Or as a confused James Bond might say, "stirred, not shaken!"

end of each day—*the* sign of expertise. The branch manager, wanting to reward my accomplishment, assigned me to train a new teller, twenty years my senior, who had come from another bank—a woman who had used up her lifetime supply of smiles in the job interview.

Armed with a new college degree and thirty-four days' experience, I thought I was hot stuff! But my freshman attempt at peer mentoring came to a screeching halt when I placed a loud "but" at the end of a compliment about her work. She rose to her feet and coldly looked me over from head to toe. "Young man, you can never boss me! I was bossing when you were a gleam in your father's eye." With that announcement, she marched into the branch manager's office and demanded a transfer to another branch. I never dreamed that a single word—"but"—could so powerfully render an effort ineffective.

Conditional affirmation ("Patsy, you're doing a great job, *but. . .*") has the effect of erasing the affirmation in the mind of the protégé. Also, because the critique now sounds parental, power and status issues are raised. So what do you do? Separate praise and criticism. If your goal is to praise, praise. If your goal is to criticize, criticize. Mixing both in the same sentence or session can turn a compassionate pat on the back into a controlling kick in the pants—especially when your protégé is your peer.

If your goal is to praise, praise. If your goal is to criticize, criticize. Mixing them can turn a compassionate pat on the back into a controlling kick in the pants.

NEVER RESIST RESISTANCE

One of the greatest lessons students of judo learn is never to resist resistance; instead, they learn to divert the energy of resistance to other uses. When you meet resistance with resistance, the barriers become more rigid, the heels of learning dig deeper into the ground of power, and growth comes to a screeching halt.

Judo teaches students to use their opponent's energy by joining it and guiding it to a new place. Similarly, in a mentoring situation, you will do better to accept the learner's resistance and seek to learn from it. Pursue it, solicit it, and get it into the light of day by showing no fear of it. Treat conflict as a neutral force that can be applied to learning. Accept it as unresolved tension that needs to be understood to be channeled in a positive direction.

STRIVE FOR RECIPROCAL LEARNING

Pursue equality in your relationship. Learning happens best when it occurs on a level playing field. If your protégé sees you as a fellow learner (rather than as an "I'll show you" smarty pants), there is greater potential for a partnership. With partnership comes acceptance, joint contribution, and growth.

Seek something your peer-protégé knows that you would like to learn, and couple your mentoring with protégéing. Better still, pursue an area in which you both want to learn. One of my partners, Ron Zemke, has been an important mentor of mine for over twenty years; we've been business

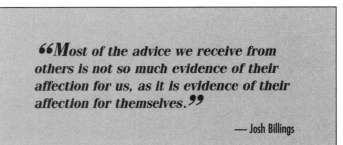

Most of the advice we receive from others is not so much evidence of their affection for us, as it is evidence of their affection for themselves.

— Josh Billings

partners for ten. He makes mentoring me a personal joy because he is just as interested in being mentored. As I get to be the student, I also get to be the teacher. The reciprocity is rarely a perfectly balanced fifty-fifty. Healthy relationships in all areas of life are sixty-forty one week and forty-sixty the next. Over time, however, the give-and-take clearly reflects a fair balance.

Peer mentoring offers both special rewards and special challenges. The secret to success lies in taking what is ostensibly an equal relationship and managing the exchange of wisdom so that it maintains and honors that equality. Focusing on humility, sincere consideration, authentic affirmation, and balance can foster an exchange that brings delight to both mentor and protégé.

IV

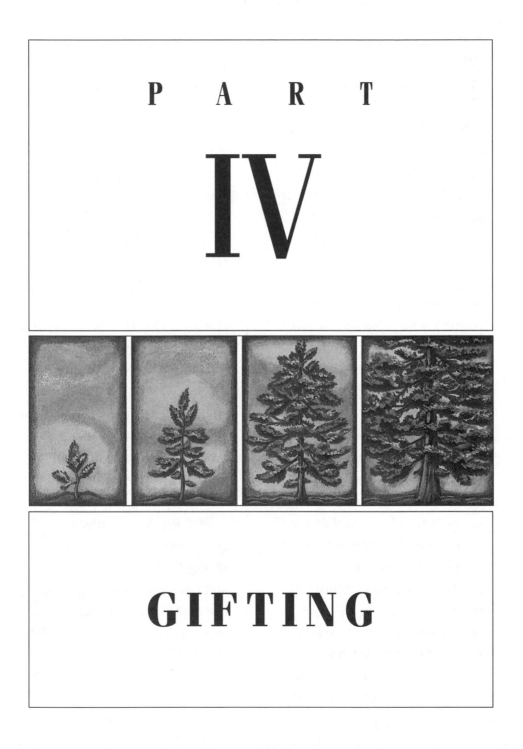

GIFTING

I grew up on a small farm in South Georgia. I made most of my annual spending money mowing lawns in the summertime. (The concept of an allowance was not invented until 1962—after I left home!) I got a dollar for a regular yard and two dollars for a large yard. My grandparents had a two-dollar yard. I always got excited when it was time to mow their yard because there weren't a lot of two-dollar yards where I lived.

In the summer of 1954 we had a major drought, the kind of rainless condition that makes yards go into a don't-grow, just-survive mode. I was looking at a bleak school year economically. Toward the end of that summer, my grandmother called and said, "Chip, I want you to mow my yard." I was thrilled! I don't think it really needed mowing, but she seemed to sense my cash shortage and came to my rescue. I mowed her yard and met her on the back porch to collect my two dollars. Instead she handed me a five-dollar bill and said the most generous words I had ever heard: "Keep the change!" It changed my relationship with my grandmother— and I kept the change until she passed away at eighty-four.

After you extend the invitation to the mentoring process (through surrendering) and establish the relationship (through accepting), the platform is now set for the main event: gifting. Essentially, the protégé is in the presence of the mentor for the gifts the mentor can offer. However, the way this encounter is managed can make a dramatic difference both in the quality of the learning and in how well it is retained.

Gifting is an expression of generosity. It is different from giving. "Giving" often implies some reciprocal toll; "gifting" is the bestowing of assets without any expectation of return. The spirit of gifting changes the nature of the relationship from *guilt-based indebtedness to joy-driven partnership. And the alliance of mentor and protégé is far healthier when the pleasure of teaching exactly matches the enchantment of learning.*

Why is this so?

Relationships are healthier when there is some reciprocity or balance—not perfectly fifty-fifty, but some appropriate level of fairness. Most learner-takers, however, feel indebted to their mentor-givers: "She gives so much, and I have nothing to give in return." This is how guilt, liability, and obligation get started. Such anxieties, no matter how subliminal, get in the way of effective development. The learner has no tangible way to balance the relationship, at least in the short run. So it is important for the mentor to show that she has been amply rewarded by the opportunity to mentor and the pleasure inherent in the process. Reciprocity is the mentor's saying indirectly to the protégé, "My payment is the sheer joy I get from seeing you grow and learn. You owe me nothing."

The next four chapters will explore several dimensions of gifting. The opening chapter in this part zeroes in on balance as an important contribution to the learning process. The closing chapter addresses a challenging aspect of mentoring: how are gifts bestowed when the learner is not present to receive them?

THE BLUEBIRDS' SECRET

The Gift of Balance

BLUEBIRDS are wonderful mentors! There's a bluebird house on an oak tree six feet from our bedroom window. The same pair of bluebirds returns each spring to build, populate, and empty a nest in it. This past spring, their parenting process caused me to reflect on how instructive bluebird flying lessons could be for mentors. Bluebirds don't just hatch their eggs and depart. They act as mentors in getting a young bird from the security of the birdhouse to the serenity of flight.

Effective mentoring is especially crucial in this era of rapid change and increasing organizational complexity. Employees who don't continue to grow will be unable to cope, adapt, and succeed. Those who wait for the next opening in a much-needed training class may be quickly left behind. In times like these, the mentor becomes a key source for real-time employee learning. But combining an in-charge role with an "in-sight" goal calls for balance—and that's where the bluebirds come in.

FIND THE TEACHABLE MOMENT

How does the bluebird know when its fast-growing offspring is ready to be pushed from the nest? Bluebirds have genetically coded weaning instincts and an innate sense of timing. They watch for certain subtle signs of maturity: restlessness, wing strength, the eagerness of the infant's lunge toward the birdhouse exit even when there's no worm dangling from mama's beak, and a whole bunch of other stuff they haven't told the bird researchers.

One key to their attentiveness is the way they take different viewpoints. Bluebird parents often perch some distance away and call out to the baby bluebird, as though to gauge reaction time—how fast does Junior respond to the chirp? A parent bluebird might perch atop the birdhouse and peer down through the entrance hole. While it would obviously be easier to observe from inside, the bluebird knows that to get a true picture the comfortable and familiar close-up examination must be balanced with views from more dangerous and diverse angles and conditions.

> **66 Well timed silence hath more eloquence than speech. 99**
>
> — M. T. Tupper

Baby bluebirds and protégés need teachable moments. One of the chief complaints protégés make about their mentors is, "He was not on hand when I really needed him." This key, often brief opportunity is sometimes called "the teachable moment." The timing of this moment is important: it's a combination of the learner's readiness to learn, the quickness with which learning can be applied, and the special conditions likely to foster or support learning.

So what should a mentor do to match teaching with timing? And how does the mentor demonstrate the right amount of attention? Too much attention can leave the protégé feeling smothered; too little can make her feel abandoned.

▶ Stay vigilant for every opportunity to foster discovery. Whenever you communicate with the protégé, ask yourself, Is there learning that can be derived from this?

▶ Keep a lookout for signs of protégé apathy, boredom, or dullness, any of which may indicate a plateau in learning.

▶ Ask "A" and listen for "B." For example, ask the question, "How would you describe the challenge in your job?" but listen for the answer as if you had asked, "How would you describe your growth or learning deficit in your job?" It is far easier for protégés to talk about being challenged or not being challenged than to discuss a learning deficit.

▶ From a distance, watch protégés at work. As you watch your birdhouse from a distant railing, keep in mind that your goal is to determine whether it might be a good time to intervene as a mentor.

The challenges for all mentors are "When does too much support become rescuing?" and "When does too little support become a sign of callousness?"

SUPPORT WITHOUT RESCUING

The morning the baby bluebird took that first clumsy flight from the birdhouse to the nearest bush, both parents were on

Mentor Scale and Balance

The Mentor Scale can be helpful in examining the issue of balance. Below are a few cautions based on your score on the Mentor Scale.

Sociability

Low: You may have a propensity to leave the protégé feeling abandoned. Provide more attention. Don't be so quick to mentor and run. Demonstrate your interest in and concern for your protégé.

High: You may have a tendency to smother the protégé by overassisting. Remember: too much help can be as great a liability as too little. Back off a bit and give the protégé a wonderful opportunity: the chance to fail, and thus to learn.

Dominance

Low: You may leave the protégé feeling betrayed. When he gets no guidance at all, the protégé can feel alone and anxious—especially early in the relationship. Let self-direction happen, but don't abdicate. Hang in there with the learner until you conclude he has wings strong enough to fly on his own.

High: You may have an inclination to rescue. Remember that growth comes through discovery and insight. Too much control can deprive the learner of the opportunity to find them on her own. Let go of the reins and give her a bit more slack.

Openness

Low: You may cause the protégé to feel anxious, particularly early in the relationship. Guarded behavior begets guarded behavior. Remember, your timidity, caution, and reserve will only amplify similar feelings in the protégé. Take interpersonal risks, lighten up, communicate your feelings. It will help break the ice and relax your protégé.

High: When you are too open too soon, you can make the protégé feel apprehensive. You set a standard that learners may feel unable or unwilling to model and match. Openness and vulnerability are positive attributes in a mentoring relationship. However, too much too soon can be overwhelming.

hand for the occasion, proud and no doubt anxious. As the wobbly fledgling took a short, awkward burst of flight, one parent was in the tree nearby providing comforting chirps of encouragement.

Suddenly, Taco (Bell), our black cat, came around the corner. Instantly, one of the parents flew within a few feet of Taco, distracting her long enough for the young bird to reach a limb safely out of range of the curious cat. It was a beautiful display of courageous selflessness by the parent, vital and well-timed support—but the student pilot was still left to do its own flying.

Mentors provide support and encouragement as protégés work to transform shaky new skills into confident mastery. The challenges for all mentors are "When does too much support become rescuing?" and "When does too little support become a sign of callousness?" Most mentors are tempted to take help to the level of interference. Too often we say, "Let me just show you how to do that!" when we should be asking, "What do you think you should do next?"

The following assemble-it-yourself statement may help you find the right balance between helpful support and unhelpful rescue.

If I were really honest with myself, I would say I tend to offer help because

- ▶ I don't want to see the protégé repeat mistakes I've made.

- ▶ I can't afford too many errors in the name of learning.

- ▶ I don't want to see the protégé hurt, embarrassed, disappointed, or discouraged.

- ▶ I need to show the protégé how competent I am.

- ▶ if I don't show the protégé how, he'll never learn or become competent.

If there is one lesson the bluebirds can offer, it is the living illustration of the teacher's courage to let the learner fail.

If there is one lesson the bluebirds can offer, it is the living illustration of the teacher's courage to let the learner fail.

Mentors, like parents, want learning to be painless, but most significant growth happens through the discomfort of grappling for skill. En route to walking and running, knees get skinned. The bluebird dived courageously at the menacing cat as the student pilot fluttered awkwardly down the backyard runway. The parent seemed to be protecting its youngster—and more: demonstrating bravery for it. Learners dare to risk when they see the teacher take risks.

There's nothing wrong with mentors showing off to protégés, as long as what they are showing is their genuineness—clay feet and all.

AVOID PERFECTION

There is one point this book will make over and over: The greatest gift a mentor can give a protégé is to demonstrate authenticity and realness. Conversely, the highest barrier to learning is an environment laced with expectations of perfection and implications of "Why can't you be as good as I am?" There's nothing wrong with mentors showing off to protégés, as long as what they are showing is their genuineness—clay feet and all. Consider the following suggestions:

▶ Tape your mentoring sessions to see if they contain controlling language: "I want you to . . . ," "You should . . . ," or the patronizing royal "we," as in "Now we must take our medicine."

▶ Listen to see whether you are taking as many interpersonal risks as the protégé in being real and open. Do you sound like an expert or a fellow learner? Would the protégé hear you as a schoolmarm or as an experienced colleague?

▶ Eliminate anything that may communicate power or distance. Mentoring from behind a desk can be far more intimidating than sitting at a forty-five-degree angle without barriers. Role or position power can be an obstacle when learning is the objective. Take steps to literally and symbolically minimize its impact.

▶ Be open to alternative views and unique interpretations. The path to excellence zigs and zags between extreme views. Help the protégé refine her view by honoring the extreme, while asking questions to encourage the discovery of a balanced, more effective position.

▶ Take the learning seriously, but not yourself. Laugh *with* your protégé, never at his mistakes. An occasional "I've made that same mistake" can melt learner apprehension and promote the risk taking needed to learn.

Our bluebirds are empty-nesters at the moment. Their fledgling has no doubt joined the world of adult bluebirds and is out hunting tasty bugs, dodging curious cats, and perhaps serving as the flight instructor for a newer generation. Like the bluebirds, the final gift of the mentor is to allow the protégé the freedom to find her own way.

THE MENTOR'S GREATEST GIFT

Passionate Connections

ARRY SMITH lost it! And he lost it in—of all places—the big-deal quarterly executive meeting. He went absolutely over the edge in his impassioned plea on some issue concerning a customer. No, he wasn't angry—but he was intense. And although he demonstrated a few gestures that would be the envy of any aspiring thespian, he didn't pound the table.

But what Larry did, in his out-of-control passion, clearly crossed all normal bounds of rationality and routine board-room decorum—and engaged the hearts and commitment of every person in the meeting. All were truly moved. People may be instructed by reason, but they are inspired by passion. It *did* make a difference. Stuff happened!

Larry Smith is the real-life vice president of service management for PKS Information Services in Omaha, Nebraska. The scene was a typical meeting at PKS, where rationality is routinely relegated to the sidelines and people, particularly senior officers, are encouraged to passionately connect with others on any issue, especially a customer issue. PKS is one of the winners in the information services outsourcing business. Just as there was David talk in Goliath Land after stones were thrown, PKS is no doubt regularly the subject of water cooler conversations at EDS, IBM, and other major competitors. And for good reason: the folks at PKS are tops at what they do.

The "Larry loses his cool" incident at PKS led me to reflect on the true meaning of contemporary leadership and mentoring. I thought about how so much mainstream corporate culture is invested in control, consistency, and keeping one's cool. And I thought about how little these values had anything to do with the fervor, spirit, and passion with which people who love their work achieve success.

People don't brag about their rational marriages, their reasonable hobbies, or their sensible vacations. In-control behavior is nowhere to be seen when Junior is rounding third base. Even taciturn fishermen have things to say when the cork goes under and the cane pole bends double. But somehow all that ardor becomes an unwelcome and embarrassing aberration within corporate walls. And the closer you get to mahogany row, the less tolerance you find for sounds of the heart.

I also thought about how liberating it was for everyone in that room when Larry lost his cool. Were we uncomfortable? Yes! Did we wonder, Where the heck is this going? Yes! But we all felt momentarily in touch with real life. It made me remember the poem about the moth fatally attracted to the flame but

People may be instructed by reason, but they are inspired by passion.

"feeling more alive in that final moment than I have ever felt in my life." Shelby Latcherie, Julia Roberts's character in the movie *Steel Magnolias*, echoed this sentiment when, as an expectant mother eager to give birth but facing potentially fatal complications from diabetes, she chose "thirty minutes of wonderful" over a lifetime of "nothing special."

Great mentors are not always rational beings; they are often flame seekers. They give passionate birth in the face of threatening circumstances. The biography of almost every great leader who ever faced the potential of bodily harm in pursuit of a cause communicates a consistent theme: *Why* we were there played so loud in my ear I never really heard *what* might happen *because* we were there. These leaders put issues such as personal safety and control on some emotional back burner and let passion lead. We know Larry; he's not an irrational, illogical person. Yet somehow we trusted his passion as much as his reason—perhaps more.

The closer you get to mahogany row, the less tolerance you find for sounds of the heart.

PASSION IS HONEST

Passion is more honest than reason. To be sure, logic is more elegant, more sensible, and surely more prudent. And one feels far safer and calmer with the rational; predictability never makes the heart race. Passion leaves us fearing an on-the-edge, unanticipated outcome. It also makes us feel free, alive, and somehow real and whole. And when leaders evoke that feeling in us, we are somehow more energized, more like a knight ready for battle.

When I was an infantry unit commander in Vietnam, young men went into battle daily with no knowledge of the complex sociopolitical ramifications of the war. Yet these men were ready to die. For what? For duty, honor, and country. Can any cause be more illogical and amorphous? What's the sense of charging an entrenched sniper who will almost certainly add you to his body count? For duty? What's the rationale behind bleeding to death in a rice paddy far from Cincinnati or Cheyenne or Charlotte? Honor? What brought GIs from Alamo, Hoxie, and Sterling the silver star and the distinguished service cross? It was passion, not reason. Action was spurred by the spirit of the moment, not the logic of geopolitics.

What would you die for at work?

"Die for?" you ask. "Are you insane?"

Consider this: Is not business welfare as important to our global survival as national pride?

"Whoa!" you say. We can't survive the chaos of unbridled emotion and the confusion of out-of-control desire. What would the stockholders say? After all, is it not the role of our leaders to bring forth grace under pressure, to keep their cool when all around them are losing theirs? Should leaders not strive to be more anchor than sail? More rudder than oar?

No! And again—No!

We have missed the boat on what it means to be a leader and a mentor. The world, the organization, and the situation offer far more predictability than is required. Leaders do not have to *add* order, sanity, rationality, or logic. Every seam of business life is stretched to bursting with those qualities. On the contrary, a truly sane leader, one faced with the daunting task of stirring the troops to action, fosters insane passion. A memorable leader calls up in each of us a visit to the ragged edge of brilliance and the out-of-the-way corner of genius.

When we feel inspired, incensed, ennobled, we have visited the magic realm of passion. Typically, we return from that realm renewed, revitalized—and perhaps a bit embarrassed at discovering our unsuspected talents. And when a leader has had a hand in showing us the way to that realm, we return with a new sense of partnership.

When we feel inspired, incensed, ennobled, we have visited the magic realm of passion. And when a leader has had a hand in showing us the way to that realm, we return with a new sense of partnership.

PASSION IS INVITATIONAL

"There is an energy field between humans," wrote *Love and Will* author and philosopher Rollo May. "And when a person reaches out in passion, it is usually met with an answering passion." Passionate connections invite passionate responses, and leadership and mentoring are fundamentally about invitation.

Ask twenty people to name the greatest leader of all time. Sure, you might get a general or two, but the list will probably have more leaders who stirred their followers with fire than leaders who motivated with reasoning. The names John Kennedy, Winston Churchill, Martin Luther King Jr., Mother Teresa, and Albert Schweitzer are not connected so much with rationalism as with passion; nor

> *One person with passion is better than forty people merely interested.*
>
> — E. M. Forster

are Southwest Airlines' CEO Herb Kelleher, Bruce Nordstrom, Ritz Carlton's Horst Schulze, or the late Sam Walton. The great leader's invitation to action is his own passion.

In his powerful new book *Leading Change*, James O'Toole finds a strong case for passion in his study of a modern American industrial prophet. Why were Edwards Deming's concepts of quality so late to be embraced by his own country? Was it Yankee arrogance? Why did the Japanese embrace Deming and his views early, showing him an almost godlike reverence, while his own country treated him like a half-mad geezer?

Deming connected passionately with the Japanese people. O'Toole quotes the director of the Japanese Union of Scientists and Engineers: "[Deming] loved Japan and the Japanese from his own heart. The enthusiasm with which he did his best for his courses still lives and will live forever in the memory of all concerned. . . . Featuring all these educational activities was his deep love and high humanness." When he returned to the United States, he expressed not love but disdain for those who formerly had shunned his views. No Japanese ever described Deming as ornery or difficult to work with—yet most American executives found Deming's attitude toward them gruff, inflexible, sometimes callous. O'Toole hypothesizes that Deming's own demons may have been the greatest obstacle to getting his brilliant concepts of quality embraced in his own homeland.

One of my partners, Ron Zemke, and I checked into a mid-town New York hotel one evening. I approached a desk clerk with a mile-wide smile and a jovial disposition. Remembering my late mother-in-law's line, "A stranger is a friend you haven't met yet," I made twenty seconds of small talk with the desk clerk, calling him by his name, which I saw on his uniform jacket. My partner was at the tail end of a head cold and had just gotten off an eight-hour flight. He was, to put it diplomatically, in a rather somber mood and had little to say to the desk clerk at his end of the counter.

Our plan was to go to our respective rooms, drop our luggage, and rendezvous in my room before dinner. And that's what we did. Ron dropped his luggage in his room, then came across the hall to my—*suite!*

"How did you get a suite?" he asked with obvious irritation.

"My Southern accent!" I replied.

The truth obviously lay in the fact that I took the time—a whole twenty seconds—to connect with my desk clerk. And what a difference it made: seventy-five square feet, Ron would say with mild bemusement. But the story doesn't end there. When we returned from dinner, my message light was on: my desk clerk had called to make sure my room was satisfactory. Ron's message light was not on. Passion is invitational.

PASSION IS A "DASHBOARD SPECIAL"

When I was a teenager, one of my classmates, Charles Holland, worked part time at the soda fountain of The Longhorn, the local after-school, after-movie, after-ballgame hangout. Charles invented a drink he called a "Dashboard Special." It had a base of "co-cola" (as we referred to Coke® back then) to which he added a shot of every syrup he had in his soda fountain—chocolate, butterscotch, vanilla, cherry, everything. It was not very tasty, but it became the local symbol for daring and bold.

When someone was "feeling his oats," he would say, "Gimme a Dashboard Special." It wasn't a macho thing, but a bold, "go for it" move—a passionate option.

Passion takes the plain vanilla out of encounters. It's a Dashboard Special leap into relationships. And it is magical! W. H. Murray, in his book *The Scottish Himalayan Expedition,* wrote: "Until one is committed, there is hesitancy, the chance to draw back, always ineffectiveness. The moment one definitely commits oneself, then Providence moves, too. All sorts of things occur to help one that would never otherwise have occurred." Goethe called it "boldness" and said, "Whatever you can do, or dream you can, begin in boldness. Boldness has genius, power, and magic in it." And the philosopher Hegel wrote, "We may affirm absolutely that nothing great in the world has been accomplished without passion."

Protégés, like all partners, need passionate connections. Leaders who lead from the heart awaken boldness in others. They build a relationship platform that raises everyone to a higher level. Confederate General Thomas J. Jackson was never again called "Tom" after someone spotted him directing defenses on the battlefield at Bull Run and remarked, "There stands General Jackson like a stone wall." His troops came to be known for the same spirited, never-say-die passion in combat. And who can forget the same phenomenon among leaders named Martin, Mahatma, and Susan B.? Reason instructs, but passion inspires.

Why are you here on this earth, in this role, at this time? What difference will your being here make? What legacy will you leave behind? Will you be forgotten for what you maintained or remembered for what you contributed? Imposing mountains are climbed, culture-changing movements are started, and breakthrough miracles are sparked by leaders who transcended rationalism and prudence, letting their spirit soar from within. Order the Dashboard Special for Larry Smith—and have one yourself!

Leaders who lead from the heart awaken boldness in others. They build a relationship platform that raises everyone to a higher level.

MENTORING ON THE RUN

White-Water Wisdom

SPEED: it is both the genie and the ogre for today's supervisors. Some thrive on it; some long for the olden days. Like it or not, however, warp speed (a.k.a. cycle time, just-in-time, or out-of-time) is the nature of what Tom Peters calls the Nanosecond Nineties. It will also be the character of the chaotic next decade—whatever we end up calling it.

The pace of today's business world challenges the supervisor's coaching and mentoring responsibilities. There are too many "I'll have to get back to you" responses to "Help me figure out how to" requests. The pressure to do wins out over the requirement to teach and learn. How can supervisors coach on the run? How can managers keep up with the demands of the "Time's up!" moment while making sure protégés receive the one-on-one attention, support, and tutelage they need to avoid skill obsolescence? Below are three steps you will find useful in mentoring on the move.

The result of a hit-and-run approach is likely to be complete confusion; an hour after you're gone, the employee will remember only a blur.

TAKE TIME FOR LEARNER READINESS

Great athletes always warm up, no matter how short the event. Under time pressure, many mentors tend to give short shrift to ascertaining whether the protégé is ready to learn. Lines like "Let me get right to the punch line" risk neglecting the protégé's learning needs and leaving him overwhelmed and confused. Remember the old truism that longer planning time results in shorter implementation time and less overall time? The same is true for learning.

No matter how little time you have for teaching, always take time to find out (1) the employee's immediate learning needs and goals ("What do you need to learn?"), (2) any pressing concerns that might affect *how* you would help, and (3) the employee's ideas on how you might be most helpful.

BEWARE OF "LET ME JUST SHOW YOU HOW!"

Good mentors don't rescue, they support. The temptation of most leaders under the gun is to resort to demonstration rather than supportive direction. The real motivation behind "Let me just show you how" is to get the work out while ostensibly helping the employee learn. This approach may boost short-term performance, but long-term proficiency suffers.

Does this mean that the mentor should never demonstrate a procedure? Of course not. The employee can often benefit from being shown how as she learns to do it for herself. But before you touch the keyboard, equipment, or report, ask yourself two questions: (1) Am I rescuing myself or supporting her? (2) Will my demonstration increase or decrease independence? We will explore this issue in more detail when we discuss mentoring around equipment (chapter 19).

Good mentors don't rescue, they support.

STRONG PARTS ARE BETTER THAN WEAK WHOLES

You're ten minutes away from rushing out the door to go to an important all-day meeting. One of your employees walks into your cubicle and announces, "I'm stuck on this new M60 filterator process you asked me to learn. Can you spare a few minutes to help me figure it out?" You know that it will actually take thirty or forty minutes to explain adequately; the employee has received only an overview orientation. Being late to the meeting is not an option, but you want some M60 performance today from this protégé. What do you do?

Many supervisors would give a ten-minute condensation of the forty-minute lesson and hope the employee could then muddle though. The result of such a hit-and-run approach is likely to be complete confusion; an hour after you're gone, the employee will remember only a blur. A better approach is to identify the ten-minute part of

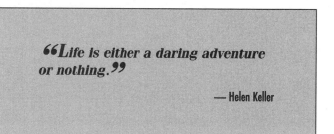

❝*Life is either a daring adventure or nothing.***❞**

— Helen Keller

your forty-minute lesson that is most crucial to getting started and cover that part thoroughly. Solid learning on a key part will create confident momentum and enable the protégé to learn the rest by himself. Competence in a limited area is better than vague awareness of the whole.

The futurists tell us that the days of "Take your time!" are over for the business world; a "Time's up!" pace, whether blessing or curse, is now essential to success. At the same time, employees must remain up to date on mastery of new skills. Superior mentors will be those who can competently tutor on the run.

MENTORING LONG DISTANCE

Remote Learning

 SAT IN THE BACK row of a large, dimly lit auditorium filled with managers from a software company. Earlier I had spoken to this audience about the myths, merits, and methods of mentoring. A bright young systems engineer manager sitting three people to my right passed me a napkin with a note: "Do you have any suggestions for how

To be effective, the buddy system must be based not just on availability but on purposeful match-making: personality matching, skill match-ing, and priority matching.

I can mentor my people in Guam, Paris, and San Juan? They feel ignored and I feel guilty."

The speaker of the moment had still a way to go in his million-slide presentation. With seventeen slides, polite applause, and closing announcements separating her napkin from my answer, I had a little time to think. I can't remember now much about what I said—she seemed satisfied—but I can remember being struck with the realization of how commonly this dilemma occurred.

We live in an era of self-directed work. Widening spans of control, downsizing, and rising numbers of employees without direct supervision have compelled leaders to supervise more and more at arm's length. Weak bosses feel relieved, their sub-ordinates freed; but strong leaders can feel guilty and their subordinates ignored. The systems engineer's dilemma is becoming familiar to more and more leaders: How do you mentor when you're not there, and won't be for a while? How do you mentor long distance?

CREATE A BUDDY SYSTEM ON SITE

When you're not there, you're not there. It's important, there-fore, to shore up other avenues for growth. A too-often-over-looked resource is the wisdom of peers. This doesn't mean going back to the old "Watch Nellie" style of yesteryear. A true buddy system carefully matches protégé learning needs with the best colleague wisdom. To be effective, the buddy system must be based not just on availability but on purposeful match-making: personality matching, skill matching, and priority matching.

So how do I get Jane to mentor John on the Tillich tech-nique when Jane and John are peers? First, hold Jane account-able for being supportive and available to mentor. Second, hold John accountable for seeking out Jane and learning the Tillich technique. Be sure to praise Jane for her mentoring, John for learning Tillich.

Easier said than done? Of course; isn't it always? Buddy systems work when we spend the effort to make them work. They require resources—especially time. Telling Jane to mentor John is great, but not if you don't cut Jane enough slack in her other duties.

PROVIDE LEARNING CARE PACKAGES

I was working with a major hotel chain, teaching a part of their week-long Lodging Leadership program. The participants were largely general managers from hotels around the world. It was lunchtime mid-week, and Steve, one of the program participants from a large hotel in New Orleans, received a large package. Many people gathered around as Steve opened the surprise. The package was filled with an eclectic assortment of items: a coffee mug, a favorite candy bar, various snacks, a package of pencils, a note pad, an inexpensive pair of reading glasses, sleeping pills, playing cards. It was from all the employees in his hotel back home. He was visibly moved. The practicality of the items was irrelevant; he had been remembered—and valued! He was suddenly reminded to do his best for his people.

Part of mentoring long distance is letting the protégé experience your concern and caring in tangible ways. An article, CD-ROM, or book on a topic of interest or need, a special job aid, or an audiotape on a work-related topic can send a powerful message that the person is remembered—and valued! Give the protégé a subscription to a magazine important to his professional growth. Place him on the routing list for growth-oriented items coming from your office.

When you are on site with the protégé, make note of small items he may not have but would find useful. Stationery and supplies may be stockroom items that can be had for the asking; unique items may take a bit more thought and planning. Could he use a rubber stamp of his business address? Is there a user list to which you could helpfully add his name? How

Part of mentoring long distance is letting the protégé experience your concern and caring in tangible ways.

would the protégé react to getting a package of post-it notes with his name printed on them? Care packages are limited only by your imagination; the best are those tailored to the protégé's individual needs, preferences, and situation.

NETWORK WITH OTHER RESOURCES TO MENTOR ON YOUR BEHALF

When you can't be there in person, send an agent on your behalf. How many old B-grade war movies have you watched in which the hard-nosed general shows a surprising soft side by sending a valued expert in to assist? "The General asked me to drop by and see if I might be able to lend a hand!" It was usually a turning point in the movie. Learning agents are allies of growth; they can fill a gap, shore up a weakness, or simply lend confidence.

When considering people resources outside your organization, find an agent who has not just expertise but status. Providing the help of a person with both special resources and unique status can send a double message: I want to help you grow; I value you. It also can be a special treat for the agent you select.

> **66**_Honesty is the cornerstone of all success, without which confidence and ability to perform shall cease to exist._**99**
>
> — Mary Kay Ash

I had the opportunity to serve as the agent for a great mentor. I was hired by a large Northeastern bank to develop a two-day training program that would be taught to supervisors at various sites by a group of carefully selected managers. The program was designed and field tested and a series of train-the-trainer sessions was conducted. Linda Burgess was the senior project leader; Phil was one of the hand-picked managers chosen to teach this new course. I got to know Phil very well during his week in training.

One day Linda called to hire me for a day. "I need your help," she began. "Phil has a particularly difficult group next month on the other side of the state, and I think he'd feel a lot more confident if you could be there the first day—sort of as his assistant."

Phil did great! He really didn't need my help. But I could see his relief when I arrived unexpectedly that morning an hour before his first participant appeared. And I learned a lot watching him find his own style in the new program.

CREATE A SELF-DIRECTED LEARNING METHOD

"The most powerful contribution teachers can make to students," human resource development guru Leonard Nadler is fond of saying, "is to help learners become their own teachers." However, the gift of self-directed learning to the protégé can pose a threat to the mentor for whom letting go means being left out, unneeded, and undervalued. It takes great courage, compassion, and caring to let the bluebird teach itself to fly. Because it is counterintuitive to you as a caring mentor, you need to take steps to ease the transition.

Tomorrow's master mentors will be enablers, not experts; supporters, not smart persons.

Meet with your far-away protégé and establish a learning plan. (The sidebar shows the key elements in a strong plan.) Check the protégé's progress at longer and longer intervals— once a month, then once every two months, then quarterly, and so forth. The goal is to wean *yourself* out of the process, not just the protégé. Make sure the strategies for learning use resources available to the protégé. Protégés who take responsibility for their own learning will show greater motivation. The old saw, "If the student hasn't learned, the teacher hasn't taught," does not apply to adults. (It doesn't apply to children either, but that's another story.)

Elements of a Learning Plan

1. My learning goal is: (e.g., I would like to develop an effective customer service survey for the customers in my area of responsibility.)

2. Resources I will likely require: (e.g., I will need to talk with the general manager at the Marriott, review the marketing research section at the library, call the customer service departments of three well-known marketing research consulting firms, etc.)

3. People I know who can assist me: (e.g., I need to talk with our organization's marketing research director.)

4. Barriers I am likely to encounter and how I might overcome them: (e.g., I have an outage report due that I need to delegate to Sam; the two-hour catering meeting needs to be shortened to one hour and everyone notified; etc.)

5. Timetable I expect to use in achieving my objective:

6. Checkoffs with my manager: (dates and times)

7. Other relevant notes on my learning plan:

Mentoring long distance will become a challenge for more and more mentors. Learning cannot always be tied to a full-time, full-access relationship. Today's work world is far from stable, regular, or planned, but learning must continue if organizations are to adapt and compete. Tomorrow's master mentors will be enablers, not experts; supporters, not smart persons. They will search beyond the old horizons to provide resources for protégés in Guam, Paris, and San Juan—as well as Galveston, Peoria, and Building Four.

P A R T

V

EXTENDING

Conversation is but carving!
Give no more to every guest
Than he's able to digest.
Give him always of the prime,
And but little at a time.
Carve to all but just enough,
Let them neither starve nor stuff,
And that you may have your due,
Let your neighbor carve for you.

— Jonathan Swift

There are limits to dialogue. This book thus far has assumed that all mentoring occurs in a high-quality conversation between a mentor and a protégé. While it is true that the mentoring process is largely a conversational proceeding, it would be shortsighted and limiting to assume that dialogue is the only path to discovery and insight.

In fact, dialogue itself can be seductive, and the relationship can be codependent. Mentor and protégé in time become very comfortable with each other. The mentor derives personal satisfaction from watching the protégé learn; this leads to more conversation, more encounters. The protégé also finds pleasure in the wisdom of the mentor and the spirit of the consultation. While comfort is clearly helpful for communication, it can be a barrier to experimentation. Both mentor and protégé look forward to the next meeting, and they ultimately become so dependent on the relationship that neither is inclined to risk losing it.

While "codependent" might seem too strong a word, even a small degree of dependency can spoil the spirit of growth. The litmus test is the emotional discomfort either party would experience if the relationship came to an end. If either party's need to end the relationship is marked by guilt or resistance, some codependency has probably infiltrated the relationship.

An effective way to avoid codependency is to extend the learning beyond dialogue. As new ways to learn become available, the protégé discovers new *routes to self-sufficiency. The ultimate extension takes the mentor completely out of the learning equation, leaving the protégé to find her own way to competence—and independence.*

The closing chapters will examine several alternatives to dialogue and conversation as the forum for learning. This part begins with a familiar learning methodology—role plays—and ends with a chapter on ways the mentor can continue to mentor a most worthy protégé—the mentor herself.

The bias of most managers is to narrow, not extend, to build loyalty rather than liberty. Consequently, as with surrendering, accepting, and gifting, this final core competence is rather counterintuitive. However, as uncomfortable as it may be for her, the greatest contribution the mentor can make to the protégé's development is to let the relationship evolve to a point at which she is no longer needed. That contribution begins with extending.

18

THE ROLE
OF ROLE PLAYS

Mentoring with Behavior Rehearsal

O ONE LIKES role-play exercises. Tell a training class that they are about to engage in a role play and you can cut the gloom with a knife. But how do you learn an interpersonal skill without some kind of reality practice? It would be like learning to fly a plane by correspondence course!

There are several reasons people don't like role plays. Trainers often misuse role plays as theatrical demonstrations: "Sandra, why don't you and Sam come up front here and role play a supervisor giving feedback to a subordinate?" Participants have to practice in front of their peers "on stage," where the cost of error is high. The point of the exercise—self-awareness—becomes lost in a painful self-consciousness. Few interpersonal skills are actually practiced in a room full of watching colleagues.

There are other reasons. Most role plays in classes are performed as trios—the "er/or" (interview-er, train-er, super-vis-or), the "ee" (interview-ee or train-ee), and the observer. The person playing the "ee" role rarely acts the way the "ee" would in real life. The observer who is supposed to critique the playlet is typically untrained in how to do so. Since the observer knows she will have a turn as an "er/or," her critique is likely to be either too harsh (so she will look better by contrast) or too forgiving ("I'll be kind to you so you'll be kind to me"). The net effect is usually a large reduction in the learning value of the experience. Is it any wonder that role plays get negative reviews?

A role play is not a testing situation to demonstrate incompetence; wire the encounter for success, not assessment.

There are times when an effective mentor needs to help a protégé with an interpersonal skill. And there are occasions when the best method to learn what needs to be learned is through some kind of behavior rehearsal. Setting up, conducting, and critiquing a role play can be a powerful skill for an effective mentor.

SETUP IS ESSENTIAL

Too often role plays are long on acting and short on rehearsal. To make role plays effective in enhancing learning, the mentor needs solid, careful preparation. Start by focusing on the specific interpersonal or judgment-making skill the protégé needs to learn. "To learn how to handle a hostile associate who failed to get the work assignment he had hoped to get" is far more targeted than "to improve conflict resolution skills." As the old adage goes, If you don't know where you're going, any road will get you there.

The focus can generally be defined as a problem or dilemma. It might be how to tell an employee she is going to be outplaced, or communicating a major disappointment to a work team, or admitting a significant error to a colleague negatively affected by that error. The key is to be clear about the interpersonal hurdle that is to be overcome.

> **"There is no wisdom like frankness."**
>
> — Benjamin Disraeli

Second, describe the factors or "noise" that might be associated with the dilemma. Telling an employee she is being outplaced is one thing, but doing so with a hard-working, long-term employee with limited-transferable or low-demand skills during a time of high unemployment is a horse of a different color. To make the role play realistic, both players must be aware of the real-life complications the protégé is likely to encounter.

Outline the behaviors to be practiced. Review actions conducive to excellence. This is not a testing situation to demonstrate incompetence; wire the encounter for success, not assessment. Here's how it might go:

Mentor: "Remember, Joe, keep your voice low but forceful. Eye contact is also important. And if you lean forward, do so slowly. What else are you planning to work on?"

Protégé: "I also need to remember to keep my body posture open. I tend to cross my arms when I get tense. I'll need to practice not doing that, especially when I get nervous or anxious. I think I'm ready, Jane."

Notice that in this dialogue the mentor and protégé participate equally in identifying the most important behaviors to rehearse. This is not play-acting or theater. It is a person trying out behaviors that can be used in a future interpersonal encounter—not to learn a script, catchwords, or clever phrases, but as a dress rehearsal for discovering traps or likely errors and building confidence for the main event.

ALLOW DRAG TIME

It's important to allow the learner plenty of time to get into the role play. The unrealistic component of role play is that, like a time machine, it drops us abruptly into another world. Life may be unexpected, but in real life we don't experience tomorrow before we get through today. Give the protégé some drag time to get accustomed to the flow and feel of the role play.

John Wayne once remarked that he enjoyed movie making a lot more than stage work because of one simple word—cut! Life is like a stage: the curtain goes up and you're on. Learning is more like movie making; you can always yell "cut" when a scene is not going to your liking, and reshoot it.

A component of drag time is letting the protégé know that "cut" is permissible—not the word, necessarily, but the freedom on both sides of the role play to say, "Let's do that again." Remember, this is not the real McCoy; this is practice, a dress rehearsal for life in the organization. Allowing maximum elbow room to experiment is central to effective learning.

MAKE FEEDBACK CONSTRUCTIVE

The key to learning or refining an interpersonal skill is for the mentor to act as a mirror, not a judge. After the behavior practice, couch your feedback in descriptive language, not evaluative language. "You interrupted me four times before I finished" is much easier to hear and use than "You didn't listen well."

Try to express all feedback in terms of specific, observable actions; as Sergeant Joe Friday used to say on *Dragnet,*

"Just the facts, ma'am." Focus on information you believe the protégé values. Feedback that is effective accomplishes two things: it reinforces effective behaviors and it suggests improvements for the next time. This keeps skill development from becoming simply trial and error. Immediately following the role play, ask the protégé to comment first on her behavior.

PRACTICE, FEEDBACK, PRACTICE

The way most training-session role plays run is this: Two people role play, a third person observes. The observer offers feedback, critique, and suggestions for improvement. Then the players rotate roles. There's one major problem with this formula: if too much time elapses before a player can apply the feedback he receives, he may forget key points.

The best way to practice any interpersonal skill is try it, get feedback, and try it again immediately, using the feedback. After the initial role play and feedback, encourage the protégé to summarize actions he plans to work on improving. Help the learner choose a few key improvements, rather than many. As with eating an elephant, the one-bite-at-a-time approach works best.

After planning the follow-up role play, give the protégé a chance to do the role play again, incorporating the feedback. Keep repeating the process until he is on the way to mastery.

REVIEW, RENEW, REFINE

The role-play learning process does not end with a single session. Put the experience on the agenda at a later meeting, after the protégé has had an opportunity to try out her new skills in real life. Start the review by asking the protégé to describe her experience in using her new skills. Find out what worked, what was most difficult, what area caused her the most anxiety, what new aspects she needs to improve.

Learning is like movie making; you can always yell "cut" when a scene is not going to your liking.

This may be another opportunity to role play the skill to be learned with an eye to refining it. As she approaches mastery, the protégé's confidence will grow. A new opportunity to role play lets the protégé confirm her skills, bolstering her confidence and self-esteem.

Role plays are not about playing. They are a serious and useful way to acquire important interpersonal skills and self-assurance. Even if the protégé has the skills, using reality practice as a dry run can enhance confidence. As a sounding board, the mentor can extend learning far beyond the mentor-protégé dialogue.

19

DON'T TOUCH THAT DIAL

Mentoring around Equipment

HEN WE THINK of mentoring, we usually think of talk. Conversation and
dialogue are, it is true, the principal
tools mentors and protégés use in the
learning process. However, mentoring
can also be used when learning how to
operate equipment. When this is the
case, how much difference does it make
in the mentoring relationship? Plenty!

The introduction of this third element—an inanimate object—can necessitate surprising changes in the mentor's role and behavior.

MACHINE RULES

This book has offered plenty of guidelines but few hard and fast rules—on the principle that when the philosophy is clear, absolute rules constitute overkill. As we will see, that is not the case with machine mentoring. Below are rules important in combining machine learning with mentoring magic.

Do not touch the protégé's equipment

Some mentors have a tendency to reach over the shoulder of a protégé and show her what to do. This tendency should be suppressed. Reaching over the protégé's shoulder is an infringement of her space and actions and is more likely to interrupt learning than to facilitate it.

Give the big picture before going into the details

Protégés need to understand the objective before they can be expected to take action to achieve it. That is, they need to know where they're going before they start out. When a protégé understands the reason for using a particular approach, she is better able to relate procedures to applications.

Avoid patronizing remarks

Some "user-friendly" programs are designed to respond in ways that the learner may see as patronizing. For example, one computer program asks the learner to type in his name and then responds by saying, "That's good, John. You typed your name in as directed." If at all possible, avoid such programs, and certainly avoid using patronizing language. There is a large difference between patronizing and encouraging.

Jack Gamble on Mentoring around Equipment
("Mentoring in Action" Revisited)

A few weeks after Jack and Tracy's get-acquainted meeting, an Ulmer-1911 machine was delivered. Jack had been Ulmer qualified for a few years and had gone back to Wisconsin twice for refresher training. Tracy had heard about but never operated the machine and was eager to learn. Late one afternoon Jack and Tracy sat down for the first time at the console of the 1911.

"Before we start," Jack began, "I want to find out what you know about this machine." He listened as Tracy described the machine's purpose and what it could produce. "I see you've done your homework," he said proudly. Tracy smiled.

Jack continued: "Think of this machine as an extension of your right arm and imagine what it would feel like to have that arm ten feet longer than the other. Not only does hand-eye coordination change, but you're bound to feel awkward. Expect that same sensation with the Ulmer-1911."

Tracy began to feel a bit less apprehensive. "Are you going to show me how it works?" she asked, her impatience beginning to show.

"I was just like you," Jack teased, "as anxious as a long-tailed cat in a room full of rocking chairs." Tracy grinned and took a deep breath. "However," Jack continued, "it will be better for you to run this machine than to watch me run it. Just looking at the center screen, what do you think is the first step?"

Tracy quickly responded, "I'd say keying on command six and moving the dugen switch to ninety degrees."

"Great choice!" Jack answered. "And what is your objective in taking that route?"

The lesson continued until Tracy was operating the Ulmer fairly proficiently. The only time Jack touched the equipment was after Tracy had taken a series of incorrect steps and gotten so far off the starting point that she needed help in getting back. Jack's goal was to guide her thinking and understanding more than her operating and remembering.

Train the protégé to think, not just do

Be sure that the protégé understands the work-related reasons for everything she does before asking her to do it. If you focus on simply following instructions, you don't prepare her to exercise judgment. Without the capacity to judge, she will not be able to function in situations outside the normal operation of the equipment.

We have all suffered at the hands of people who don't think but just follow the rules (or instructions) whether they make sense or not. A friend of mine received a traffic ticket for going five miles per hour over the speed limit in the middle of the night while taking his injured son to the hospital emergency room. Although there was no one else on the road, the officer insisted: "Rules are rules." Teach your protégé to be effective, not an unthinking robot.

Curb jargon

Use technical terms sparingly, and use only those the protégé needs in order to learn. Do not show off by using jargon. A true mentor does not have to rely on technical terms but can explain in a way that the nontechnical protégé can understand easily.

Be patient

The protégé may suffer and express frustration, and that is perfectly acceptable. However, keep your own frustration under control. When you're helping people learn, patience is golden.

Use leading questions

Ask a series of leading questions that help the protégé discover the proper sequence of action and, hence, arrive at a proper answer. This procedure is inappropriate in mentoring that does not involve equipment, where it can be seen as disrespectful, patronizing, and manipulative; it often causes protégés to tune out or, in some cases, to rebel openly. But this method is entirely appropriate in equipment mentoring because it aligns the protégé's thought processes and puts him in sync with the way the equipment works.

The leading-questions method is not easy to use, but with practice you can become skilled in it. Here are the steps:

1. Identify the procedure the protégé is trying to learn.

2. Determine the proper sequence of actions that will help the protégé reach the learning objective.

3. Ask a series of questions that will help the protégé discover this proper sequence.

Teach your protégé to be effective, not an unthinking robot.

If the protégé encounters a problem, you can do one of four things:

1. Ignore the situation, thereby forcing the protégé to figure out the solution to the problem.

2. Ask leading questions that help the protégé discover the proper sequence of actions.

3. Tell the protégé what to do and why it should be done.

4. Take over for the protégé and use the equipment to solve the problem.

Each of these approaches can be appropriate at different times. For example, you should ignore a protégé when you know he can solve the problem but is becoming too dependent on your help. Use leading questions when it is important for the protégé to think through the issues. Go ahead and tell the protégé what to do when it will facilitate learning and not waste his problem-solving skills.

Occasionally you should even take over. For example, if a learner has so bollixed up the equipment that to allow him to unravel it would take far too long, you may have to take charge and reset it to an appropriate starting place. Whatever you do, be aware of the reasons for using that particular method and the potential impact on the protégé.

MANAGING SWEET SORROW

Life after Mentoring

EFFECTIVE mentoring relationships are rich, engaging, and intimate. But all such arrangements must come to an end, and no matter how hard we may try to avoid it, every ending has a bittersweet dimension. As Shakespeare so eloquently reminds us, "Parting is such sweet sorrow." As you and your protégé reach the end of your partnership, how do you manage "farewell" with a focus on "well"?

GOING FOR GROWTH

You would be remiss in your duties as a mentor to make the parting an occasion for lingering regret. Healthy mentoring relationships use separation as a tool for growth. Below are several ideas for gracefully and constructively ending a mentoring relationship.

Celebrate with fanfare and stories

Celebration need not be a party with band and banner; it can be as simple as a special meal together, a drink after work, a peaceful walk in a nearby park. The point of celebration, however, is to mark the end of the mentoring relationship. Celebration is a rite of passage, a powerful symbol of closure and of moving on to the next learning plateau.

In a workshop I conducted for a well-known West Coast software manufacturer, a manager mentioned that he had been getting reports from other managers that supervisors who transferred from his department seemed to take longer than usual to adjust to their new supervisory roles. It was beginning to hurt his reputation within the organization as a supplier of competent talent. I asked him to play back in reverse the events leading from his supervision to their new roles. It quickly became clear that their relationships with him never came to a formal end— they simply stopped. Later, when he began including the ritual of a celebratory closure on their last day under his supervision, the adjustment problems vanished.

> *Communicate unto the other person that which you would want him to communicate unto you if your positions were reversed.*
>
> — Aaron Goldman

Celebration should be rich in compliments and stories, laughter and joy. Your protégé graduate needs your blessing more than your brilliance, your good wishes more than your warnings. Avoid the temptation to lay on one last caution. Your kindest contribution will be a solid send-off with gifts of confidence, compassion, and consideration.

Solidify learning with nostalgia

When I left NationsBank (then NCNB) in 1979 to form a management consulting firm, Chuck Cooley, my boss and mentor of eight years, treated me to breakfast at a nearby site he and I had used countless times for mentoring meetings. He asked me two questions, both important in our parting and my growth: Whom would I recommend as my successor, and why? and What were the primary lessons I had learned over the eight years? His second question was his gentle way of getting me to reflect on how far I had come: from a green assistant training director to a seasoned director of management and organization development. Not willing to rely solely on my memory, he repeatedly interjected "Remember the time when . . . ?" stories. The departure was peaceful and complete.

Lace your final meetings with opportunities to remember, reflect, and refocus. Let your recall questions bridge the discussion toward the future; merely reminiscing can mire the meeting in melancholy. Listen to your protégé with the devotion you would give *your* mentor. Honor your mature protégé with respect and recognition. After my last meeting with Chuck I stood taller than at my college graduation. He paid me homage by honoring my development.

Let time pass before follow-up

The quickest route to delivering a message of dependence is to follow up with a protégé too soon after departure. Wait a week or more before calling or visiting. Setting your relationship free takes space and time. Should you follow up at all? Absolutely! Partners follow up on partners. The key is, not too quickly. Allow weaning time.

Let your protégé be his own person. There may be times when a former protégé is being honored and you will feel the urge to share the limelight. I once had a professor who always wanted to share the credit when one of his students achieved

Celebration should be rich in compliments and stories, laughter and joy.

some award. While pride was obviously a part of his response—"I was his major professor"—the action tended to keep his former protégé stuck in the "I'm still his student" position. Let go. Move on. Celebrate the past but concentrate on the future.

Healthy mentoring relationships use separation as a tool for growth.

As rapport building is crucial to the beginning of a mentoring relationship, adjournment is equally important at its end. Letting go is rarely comfortable, but it's necessary if the protégé is to flourish and continue to grow out of the mentor's shadow. In the final analysis, the upper limit of growing is "grown," implying closure and culmination. Mark the moment by managing adjournment as a visible expression of achievement and happiness.

THE KAIZEN OF MENTORING

Learning, Learning, Learning

HE'S NOT BUSY being born is busy dying," sang folk singer Bob Dylan. Didn't know Dylan sang business songs, did you? In today's world of enterprise, "being born" is about growth, and "busy dying" is about obsolescence, reduced productivity, and unemployment. But the word most applicable to today is "busy." Learning never stops.

Directed growth begins with a look inside that includes a thoughtful examination of strengths, limitations, improvement opportunities, needs, hopes, and fears.

As they help their protégés grow, good mentors work on their own growth. They don't grow simply as role models for protégés; they grow for their own worth. Mentors most adept at self-mentoring are those who choose a wide range of avenues for learning. This final chapter is devoted and dedicated to the self-mentoring needs of mentors.

INSIDE . . .

The famous Dr. Seuss children's rhyme "inside, outside, upside down" can be prescriptive as a route to personal growth. Learning can be thought of as coming from three different directions. Directed growth begins with a close personal examination—a look *inside* that includes a thoughtful examination of strengths, limitations, improvement opportunities, needs, hopes, and fears. Ask yourself questions like those suggested by Gary Heil, Tom Parker, and Rick Tate in their book *Leadership and the Customer Revolution*:

▶ What major area have I changed my mind about in the last quarter?

▶ How long has it been since my assumptions about something important were absolutely dead wrong?

▶ When I compare the way I think this year with the way I thought last year, what is different?

▶ What have I learned this quarter that makes my actions last quarter seem less effective?

▶ Whom am I close to who thinks very differently than I do, and what have I learned from that person?

▶ How much time have I spent in the last quarter seriously questioning the way I think?

▶ What was the last skill I learned with my associates? From my associates?

▶ How long has it been since I lost an important argument with one of my associates?

OUTSIDE . . .

After you've taken a look inside, your next step is to consider *outside* resources. Where are your learning opportunities likely to be richest? Most accessible? What people, tools, supports, and permissions might you need for effective learning? What resources are going to be important to your growth? Are there resources you can borrow, trade for, buy, or get simply for the asking? Leave no stone unturned.

There is an old joke about a man who tried to escape a rising flood by climbing to the roof of his house. Rescuers came by in a boat and pleaded with the man to come with them and escape the flood. "No," said the man, "I have put my faith in the Almighty. I will be fine." An hour later another boat came by to save the man, now on the highest point of his roof as the floodwaters continued to rise. Again he refused rescue. Some time later a helicopter flew over his house and the crew tried to persuade the man, now sitting on top of his chimney, to climb the rope ladder and escape. Again the man said, "No, I have put my faith in the Almighty. Go away, I will be fine."

The man drowned. Soon he found himself at the Pearly Gates. Angrily, he confronted St. Peter. "How could you let me down? I put my faith in the Almighty and you did nothing to save me!"

> **Only the curious will learn and only the resolute overcome the obstacles to learning. The quest quotient has always excited me more than the intelligence quotient.**
>
> — Eugene S. Wilson

St. Peter looked at his clipboard and with great puzzlement responded, "I don't understand it either. According to this, we sent you two boats and a helicopter!"

. . . UPSIDE DOWN

There are many resources available for our growth. Some, however, are well disguised, requiring us to look in out-of-the-way places, turn things *upside down,* and squint to find them. What are your greatest strengths? What components of those strengths have liabilities? I have a colleague who is an excellent editor. However, this asset keeps him from writing articles he could and should write. "The critical parent in my head seems to keep me from ever completing the first paragraph." What is the least appealing hobby you might pursue? Are there aspects of that hobby that might be beneficial to you? What might you learn about yourself through mentoring a child not related to you? Do you have any weird or avant-garde friends who might teach you new perspectives?

LITTER YOUR NEST WITH NUTS

Many resources for our growth require us to look in out-of-the-way places, turn things upside down, and squint to find them.

When we had our trees trimmed, some large oak limbs contained old squirrel nests. Every nest that came tumbling to the ground revealed that the squirrels had not just stored nuts in the ground nearby, they had plenty in their nests. Learning needs the same storage system. Avoid the "out of sight, out of mind" potential by littering the world in which you live with opportunities to learn.

Is there a magazine rack in your bathroom at home? Do you have tapes in your car on a subject important to your growth? Have you used your library card in the last six months? Are there magazines you would read more often if you had a subscription? Is there always a book in progress in your briefcase or flight bag? Put a pad, pencil, and pen light beside your bed so ideas that visit you at 2:00 a.m. are not lost by dawn. Trade in watching television for a hobby that expands your mind. Trash the computer games on your laptop. Read! Write! Think!

START A LEARNING JOURNAL

Journalizing has proven to be a powerful tool for personal growth. Just as a Day-Timer helps in priority management and organization, a journal gently forces the learner to be disciplined, focused, and reflective. Like a counselor or therapist, a journal helps us transform information into understanding. As a synthesizing device, a journal extends our learning beyond predictable skills to deeper awareness and mastery.

There are countless ways to keep a journal. Go to the bookstore or office-supply store and purchase a bound, blank book to capture your journal entries. Daily (preferably at about the same time) jot down your thoughts about what you have learned, your reaction to the learning, and your plans for using it.

Journals are records for review. Once a week, review your daily entries; every month, review the previous four weeks. Coach yourself to dig deep as you analyze and assess. Note themes, patterns, and trends. Pretend you are reviewing the journal of someone you do not know. What advice would you offer? What cautions might you urge? What suggestions?

Litter the world in which you live with opportunities to learn.

SELECTED BOOKS

Writers recommend books. Surprise, surprise! Even as I list some of my favorite books, I will echo a criticism a colleague leveled at me early in my career: "Chip, you read too much and don't think enough." He was on the mark. Some of my motivation to read books was not about learning but about boasting. As you read, periodically stop and ask: What can I do with what I am learning? What are the larger, grander, deeper implications of what this book is telling me?

A word of caution about my list: Different books speak to people in different ways and at different times in their career. If you select a book, carefully read the preface, scan the content cover to cover, read a fourth of the book. If you're not drawn in, select another. If you believe you've given a book a fair chance to teach you but you're not getting a return on time invested, don't waste another minute on it.

My list of favorite books below was assembled with one purpose in mind: to help you become the best mentor you can be. Some of the books are old; most are new. Old books are worthy of a second reading. My favorite book on coaching is *How to Grow People into Self-Starters*, by my partner Dr. Tom Connellan. I still enjoy rereading *Zen and the Art of Motorcycle Maintenance*, by Robert Pirsig; popular a few years back, it taught me a lot about following the flow of relationships rather than driving them to my own ends. Max De Pree's *Leadership Jazz* offers a clear, pragmatic look at the leader as partner. I am also a fan of the work of John Gardner, particularly *On Excellence*. Jerry Harvey's *The Abilene Paradox* has always helped me get past some of the absurdity of organizational life. Finally, I would recommend that you reread *The Little Prince*, by Antoine de Saint-Exupéry; this childhood book is uniquely deep in examining the soul of mentoring.

EPILOGUE

There is some instructive irony in the fact that I wrote this book in the months surrounding my dad's departure from this world. As you learned in chapter 12, he died at age eighty-four. I suspect that for most people the death of a parent provokes reflection and reexamination. He was my first mentor. In many ways, he was my best.

Ray Bell was a quiet man; he would have set a new record for low sociability on the Mentor Scale. Despite his shyness, he was famous for his quick wit, his optimism, and his talent as a good-natured tease. He was also a deep and passionate man, capable of stirring oceans of insight with a few carefully chosen words. Ray Bell demonstrated several qualities central to great mentoring. These qualities are perhaps the touchstones for any person intent on being a catalyst for the learning of another.

JUDGMENT FREE

Daddy could be a stern taskmaster and a tough disciplinarian. When it came to performance, he was a perfectionist. He expected the best, demanded the best, and demonstrated the best. However, when the goal was learning, he shifted to a completely different style. His taskmaster side would suddenly became patient, even tolerant—and above all, nonjudgmental. When the objective was growth, my most inane question was treated as evidence of insight just waiting to happen. He never snickered at my ignorance nor scorned my naiveté. As a young man I heard a lot more expressions of "Good try!" than exclamations of "Good gracious!" Whenever I was busy working to acquire a new skill or knowledge, leeway and latitude seemed to be his specialty.

PERPETUAL CURIOSITY

Daddy asked me questions to which he did not know the answers. That always stood in stark contrast to the tendencies I witnessed in many of my friend's parents. My buddies seemed frequently to get asked questions with the slam of a spring-loaded bear trap; "Do you have any idea what time it is?" was not really a "Where did I lose my watch?" kind of question. But Daddy never used questions that way. When he asked a question, it was always in search of new learning. I came to see this as evidence of his perpetual curiosity.

On family driving trips, we stopped at every historical road sign. We had long Sunday-afternoon discussions provoked by queries such as "What do you reckon Charles Dickens meant by that?" or "I wonder what Julius Caesar might have been feeling when that happened?" He took things apart just to see how they were made. He watched squirrels build a nest, then launched into a question-filled discussion of nest-building genes and weather-sensing skills. Great mentors never stop being curious—and they unabashedly let it show.

OBVIOUS PRIDE

Ray Bell experienced life firsthand, but he experienced it secondhand as well. When my hard-won competence was displayed in some public presentation, it was as if he too were on the stage, down the court, across the field, or in the pulpit. He was noticeably proud of his children's accomplishments—and never with a credit-seeking "That's *my* boy!" possessiveness. He just seemed thrilled to see how it all worked out.

Mentors bubble over with pride when they see the effects of their mentoring relationships. They not only experience vicariously the growth of their protégés, they look for ways to bear witness to the power of learning. I often felt Daddy's pride was part "Isn't that great!" and part "Isn't that amazing!" Not that he was surprised that I could actually do what he taught; I think he was just awed by the whole process of learning. He started his professional career as a teacher, coach, and school principal. And even though he moved to other careers, among them banker and farmer, the teacher in him never got turned off. My sister, my brother, and I were the lucky students of his tutelage.

IMPECCABLE ETHICS

One very important lesson I learned from him was this: Mentoring is an ethical act. Effective mentors must be clean in their protégé dealings, not false, manipulative, or greedy. Competent mentors must be honest and consistent in their communications and actions. They must not steal their protégés' opportunities for struggle or moments of glory. Great mentors refrain from coveting their protégés' talents or falsifying their own. They honor the protégé, just as they honor the process of mutual learning.

As you and I approach the final few pages of this mentoring journey together, I will end with the *most* important lesson I learned from Ray Bell, the master mentor in my life. Dr. Malcolm Knowles taught me that a really great mentor must first and foremost love the learning. Ray Bell taught an even greater lesson: The mentor must first and last love the protégé!

ACKNOWLEDGMENTS

No one writes a book alone. Many people gather around the solo author to transform rough words on a computer screen into polished prose on a printed page. This is my opportunity to thank the many who gathered with me. The task is a bit daunting, not unlike all those Academy Award winners whom we annually watch struggle under spotlight and camera to remember all the people to thank.

There were three teams who worked on *Managers As Mentors*. The Texas production team was headed by Leslie Stephen in Austin. Leslie demonstrated late-at-night, around-the-clock commitment to this book from the very git-go. She delivered her extraordinary management talents and creative strengths in a fashion that usually felt effortless and always seemed limitless. Ray Bard, of Bard Books, Inc., gave both his perpetual belief in the book and his special vision of what it might become. Jeff Morris was the vernacular engineer who provided world-class editing. Suzanne Pustejovsky gave her vast creative genius to the design of the book and its cover. This is my fourth book with Ray and Leslie; my third with Suzanne, and my second with Jeff—enough said!

The California publishing team was led by Steve Piersanti, president of Berrett-Koehler Publishers, Inc. I know of no one who demonstrates more integrity, professionalism, and deep dedication to a true publisher-author partnership. His entire company delivers beyond-the-call-of-duty commitment. They all live their values. This is my second book with Berrett-Koehler, my third with Steve.

The Minnesota and Michigan cheerleading team included my Performance Research Associates partners: Ron Zemke, Tom Connellan, and Kristin Anderson, all authors of best-selling books. Each offered helpful suggestions, unique and partially baked ideas, and never-ending encouragement.

Finally, this book would not have happened without the emotional sustenance and ingenious inspiration of Nancy Rainey Bell. The subtitle of this book is really about Nancy. She is the best there is at building partnerships for learning. Our thirty-two-year partnership, filled with mutual mentoring, has been a joyful crucible for learning. By her unconditional love, vast intellect, and unselfish devotion, she has taught me more about partnership than any person on the planet!

To all of you: Thanks.

NOTES

Page

xi   *The ability to learn:* In Senge, p.4.

25–26   Axioms of adult learning adapted from Margolis and Bell, *Instructing for Results,* pp. 7–8. See also Malcolm Knowles's classic *The Adult Learner: A Neglected Species.*

27   *Great trainers:* Keynote speech by Malcolm Knowles at the American Society for Training and Development Senior Trainers' Symposium, Madison, Wisconsin, 1976.

39–44   The Mentor Scale was adapted from an instrument developed for *At Your Service: Designing and Delivering Top-Notch Customer-Focused Service* (packaged training program), copyright 1994 Chip R. Bell and Ron Zemke, with the permission of the publisher, Quality Resources, 902 Broadway, New York, New York 10010, phone 1-800-247-8519.

42   The FIRO-B® instrument is distributed exclusively by Consulting Psychologists Press, 3803 East Bayshore Road, Palo Alto, California 94303 (415) 969-8901, fax (415) 969-8608. An updated version, renamed *Element B: Behavior,* is available from Will Schutz Associates, Inc., P.O. Box 1339, Mill Valley, California 94942–1339, phone 1-800-462-5874, fax (415) 389-1630.

46   *Luke Skywalker is stranded:* Dialogue from the movie *The Empire Strikes Back* used courtesy of Lucasfilm Ltd. All rights reserved.

46–47   *Surrendering is the most difficult:* Bruce Fritch of Fritch and Company is in Charlotte, North Carolina.

47   *Start with practice:* Richard Furr is with Carolinas Consulting Group in Greensboro, North Carolina.

52   *Orit has that talent:* Sellers, p. 74.

75   *In a study done a few years ago:* Kram, pp. 608–625.

81   *Trust is a state of readiness . . . :* Tway, p. 8; see also University of Texas, pp. 48–52. Larry Davis is director of the Team Effectiveness Center in Austin, Texas. Duane Tway is director of CORE Consulting in Tucson, Arizona.

134   *There is an energy field:* May, p. 312.

135   *[Deming] loved Japan:* O'Toole, p. 197.

137   *Until one is committed:* Murray, p. 206.

148   *The most powerful contribution:* See *Developing Human Resources: Concepts and a Model* by Leonard and Zeace Nadler for an updated treatment of his 1970 classic.

169   *He's not busy being born . . . :* Lyric from "It's Alright, Ma (I'm Only Bleeding)." Copyright © 1965 by Warner Bros. Music, renewed 1993 by Special Rider Music. All rights reserved. International copyright secured. Reprinted by permission.

170–171   Questions adapted from Heil, Parker, and Tate, pp. 59–60. Used by permission.

REFERENCES

Bell, Chip R. *Customers As Partners: Building Relationships That Last.* San Francisco: Berrett-Koehler, 1994.

Bell, Chip R. and Ron Zemke. *Managing Knock Your Socks Off Service.* New York: AMACOM, 1992.

Castaneda, Carlos. *The Teachings of Don Juan: A Yaqui Way of Knowledge.* Berkeley: University of California Press, 1968.

Connellan, Thomas K. *How to Grow People into Self Starters.* Ann Arbor: The Achievement Institute, 1991.

Dass, Baba Ram [Richard Alpert]. *The Only Dance There Is.* Garden City, N.Y.: Anchor Press, 1974.

DeGeus, Arie. *The Living Company: Habits for Survival in a Turbulent Business Environment.* Boston: Harvard Business School Press, 1997.

De Pree, Max. *Leadership Jazz.* New York: Doubleday, 1992.

Edvinsson, Leif, and Michael S. Malone. *Intellectual Capital: Realizing Your Company's True Value by Finding Its Hidden Roots.* New York: HarperBusiness, 1997.

Greenleaf, Robert K. *Servant Leadership: A Journey into the Nature of Legitimate Power and Greatness.* New York: Paulist Press, 1977.

Harvey, Jerry B. *The Abilene Paradox and Other Meditations on Management.* New York: Lexington Books, 1988.

Heil, Gary, Tom Parker, and Rick Tate. *Leadership and the Customer Revolution: The Messy, Unpredictable and Inexplicably Human Challenge of Making the Rhetoric of Change a Reality.* New York: Van Nostrand Reinhold, 1994.

Howard, Pierce J. *The Owner's Manual for the Brain: Everyday Applications from Mind-Brain Research.* Austin, Tex.: Leornian Press, 1994.

Huang, Chungliang Al, and Jerry Lynch. *Mentoring: The Tao of Giving and Receiving Wisdom.* San Francisco: HarperCollins, 1995.

Jourard, Sidney. *The Transparent Self: Self-Disclosure and Well-Being.* New York: Van Nostrand Reinhold, 1971.

Knowles, Malcolm. *The Adult Learner: A Neglected Species* (4th ed.). Houston: Gulf Publishing, 1990.

Kram, Kathy E. "Phases of the Mentor Relationship." *Academy of Management Journal* 26:4 (1983) 608–625.

Lane, Tom, and Alan Green. *The Way of Quality: Dialogues on Kaizen Thinking.* Austin, Tex.: Dialogos Press, 1994.

Leonard-Barton, Dorothy. *Wellsprings of Knowledge: Building and Sustaining the Sources of Innovation.* Boston: Harvard Business School Press, 1995.

Margolis, Fredric, and Chip R. Bell. *Instructing for Results: Managing the Learning Process.* San Diego: Pfeiffer & Co., 1986.

Margolis, Fredric, and Chip R. Bell. *Understanding Training: Perspectives and Practices.* San Diego: Pfeiffer & Co., 1988.

May, Rollo. *Love and Will.* New York: Dell, 1969.

Murray, Margo. *Beyond the Myths and Magic of Mentoring.* San Francisco: Jossey-Bass, 1991.

Murray, W. H. *The Scottish Himalayan Expedition.* London: MacMillan & Sons, 1950.

Nadler, Leonard. *Developing Human Resources.* Houston: Gulf Publishing, 1970.

Nadler, Leonard, and Zeace Nadler. *Developing Human Resources: Concepts and a Model* (3rd ed.). San Francisco: Jossey-Bass, 1989.

Oliver, Mary. "Mockingbirds." *Atlantic Monthly,* February 1994.

O'Toole, James. *Leading Change: Overcoming the Ideology of Comfort and the Tyranny of Custom.* San Francisco: Jossey-Bass, 1995.

Peters, Tom. *Liberation Management: Necessary Disorganization for the Nanosecond Nineties.* New York: Knopf, 1992.

Peters, Tom, and Robert H. Waterman Jr. *In Search of Excellence: Lessons from America's Best-Run Companies.* New York: Harper & Row, 1982.

Pirsig, Robert M. *Zen and the Art of Motorcycle Maintenance: An Inquiry into Values.* New York: Doubleday, 1976.

Powell, John. *Why Am I Afraid to Tell You Who I Am?* (rev. ed.). Allen, Tex.: Tabor, 1990.

Rogers, Carl. *On Becoming a Person.* Boston: Houghton Mifflin, 1972.

Saint-Exupéry, Antoine de. *The Little Prince.* New York: Harcourt Brace, 1982.

Schutz, Will B. *FIRO: A Three-Dimensional Theory of Interpersonal Behavior* (3rd. ed.). Mill Valley, Calif: Schutz Associates, 1989.

Sellers, Patricia. "What Exactly Is Charisma?" *Fortune,* January 1996.

Senge, Peter. *The Fifth Discipline: Mastering the Five Practices of the Learning Organization.* New York: Doubleday, 1990.

Tuay, Duane C. "A Construct of Trust," Ph.D. dissertation, University of Texas, 1994.

University of Texas. "Leadership As Trustbuilding: Communication and Trust." Proceedings of the Eighth Annual Conference on Organizations. Lago Vista, Tex.: University of Texas, 1993.

Vaill, Peter B. *Learning As a Way of Being: Strategies for Survival in a World of Permanent White Water.* San Francisco: Jossey-Bass, 1996.

Vaill, Peter B. *Managing As a Performing Art: New Ideas for a World of Chaotic Change.* San Francisco: Jossey-Bass, 1989.

INDEX

Abilene Paradox, The (Harvey), 174
Abundance, 27–28
Accepting
  dialogues and, 93–102
  fear and, 103–110
  honesty and, 84
  listening and, 87–92
  as "mask removal," 84
  in mentoring, 11
  peer mentoring, 111–118
Achievement need, 107
Adult learning, 25–26
Advice. *See also* Feedback
  agreement on focus of, 59
  compared with feedback, 62
  goal statement before, 58–59
  role play on, 61–62
  stated in first person singular, 60
  without getting resistance, 58–60
Affirmation
  conditional affirmations, 113, 116
  partnership and, 18–19
  self-esteem and, 109
Affirmative action, xvii, 6
"Aha!" experience, 70, 75
Albee, Edward, 94
Andragogy, 25–26
Assessment on mentoring, 37–44, 72–73, 114–115,
  126
Authenticity, 101

Bain & Company, 52
Balance
  and avoidance of perfection, 128–129
  importance of, 26–27
  in Mentor Scale, 126
  and support with rescuing, 125, 127–128
  teachable moment and, 124–125
Bartering, as trap to avoid, 9–10
Bell, Bilijack, 2
Bell, Chip R., 185
Bell, Ray, 105, 175–177
Boss. *See* Leadership
Brain research, 69–70
Buddha, 75
Buddy system for remote learning, 144–145
Burgess, Linda, 146–147

Castaneda, Carlos, x
Catalyst, mentor as, 96

Celebration
  at end of mentoring relationship, 166–167
  partnership and, 18–19
Churchill, Winston, 135
Clarifying questions, 96
Clinton, Bill, 80
Closed questions, 71, 74
Codependency, 150–151
Comic, as mentoring role, 23
Communication
  advice, 57–62
  of competence, 81–82
  dialogue, 93–102
  feedback, 62–63, 65–66
  listening, 17, 87–92
  nonverbal communication, 51, 99
  questioning, 67–75, 96, 113, 162–163
Comparisons, and questioning, 71
Competence, communication of, 81–82
Compliments, as trap to avoid, 9
Computers, compared with brain, 69
Conditional affirmations, 113, 116
Confucius, 75
Connellan, Tom, 174
Control need, 108
Conversations. *See* Communication; Dialogue
Cooley, Charles J. ("Chuck"), 8–9, 167
Courage, 28
Curiosity, 70, 74–75, 175–176
Customers As Partners (Bell), 109

Davis, Larry N., 81
De Geus, Arie, xi
Deming, Edwards, 135–136
Demonstrations, 140–141
Dependence, as trap to avoid, 10
De Pree, Max, 174
Dialogue
  authenticity in, 101
  definition of, 93–94
  dos and don'ts for, 102
  extending in, 98–99
  gestures and body stance in, 99
  initiating and clarifying questions in, 96
  limits to, 150
  and mentor as catalyst, 96
  mind set and, 94–95
  paraphrasing in, 96–98
  "priming the pump" for, 95–96
  summarizing in, 98
Discovery, 70, 75

Dominance
  balance and, 126
  inquiry talents and, 72
  in Mentor Scale, 42–43, 72, 114–115, 126
  in peer mentoring, 114–115
Don Juan, x
Dramatic listening. *See* Listening
Dylan, Bob, 169

Embarrassment, over feedback, 63–65
Empathy, versus sympathy, 53
Empire Strikes Back, The 46
Empowerment, xi, 16
End of mentoring relationship, 165–168
Equipment, mentoring around, 159–163
Escalante, Jaime, 104
Ethics, 177
Evaluation, and questioning, 71
Extending
  codependency and, 150–151
  in dialogues, 98–99
  end of mentoring relationship, 165–168
  learning resources, 169–174
  in mentoring, 11, 12
  mentoring around equipment, 159–163
  role plays and, 153–158

Fear
  as educational tool, 103–104
  irrational feelings as legitimate feelings,
    105–106
  as liability in learning, 104–105
  as mirror of self-esteem, 109–110
  as rational, 105–106
  as threatened need, 106–108
Feedback. *See also* Advice
  avoidance of resentment as response to, 62,
    63–66
  and climate of identification, 63–65
  compared with advice, 62
  embarrassment about, 63–65
  feedback on, 65
  as nurturing, 66
  rationale for, 65
  on role plays, 156–157
  as straightforward and honest, 65
Feelings
  fear, 103–110
  irrational feelings as legitimate feelings,
    105–106
  passion, 28, 131–137
  receptivity for, 52–53
Fifth Discipline, The (Senge), xi
FIRO–B, 42
Focus
  of advice, 59
  listening and, 89

Follow-up on mentoring, 167–168
Fritch, Bruce, 46
Furr, Richard, 47

Gadiesh, Orit, 52
Gardner, John, 174
General to specific paraphrasing, 97
Gifting
  balance and, 123–129
  compared with giving, 120
  definition of, 120–121
  in mentoring, 11, 12
  passionate connections and, 131–137
  rapport and, 51–52
  reciprocity in, 121
  remote learning and, 143–148
  speed and, 139–142
  white-water wisdom on, 139–142
Give-and-take. *See* Dialogue
Giving, compared with gifting, 120
Goals, in advice giving, 58–59
Goethe, Johann von, 137
Grant, Hugh, 80
Greenleaf, Robert, 15

Harvey, Jerry, 174
Hegel, G.W. F., 137
Heil, Gary, 170–171
Helpfulness, as trap to avoid, 8–9
Higher-level thinking, and questioning, 71, 74
Hit-and-run approach to mentoring, 139–142
Hodges, Luther, Jr., 77–78, 80–82
Holland, Charles, 136–137
Holtz, Lou, 57
Homer, 7
Honesty
  accepting and, 84
  importance of, 27
  of passion, 133–134
Houseman, John, 103–104
How to Grow People into Self-Starters (Connellan),
    174
Howard, Pierce, 70
Humility, 80–81, 112–113

Identification, and feedback, 63–65
In Search of Excellence (Peters and Waterman), xi
Initiating questions, 96
Inquiry. *See* Questioning

Jackson, Thomas J., 137
James, William, 109
Japanese Union of Scientists and Engineers, 135
Jargon, in mentoring around equipment, 162
Jesus, 75

John XXIII, Pope, 84
Johnson & Johnson, 80
Jourard, Sidney, 84
Journal keeping, 173
Judgment-free attitude, 175
Judo, 116

Kelleher, Herb, 135
Kennedy, John, 135
King, Larry, 90
King, Martin Luther, Jr., 135
Knowles, Malcolm, 25–26, 27

Lao-tse, 75
Leader-partners, 15–19
Leadership. *See also* Mentoring
    as authority and corporate parent, xi
    celebration and, 18–19
    characteristics of good leaders, 6–7
    encouragement of risk taking in employees,
        16–17
    evolution of bossing, 13–16
    keys to effectiveness partnership, 16–19
    listening and, 17
    mentoring and, 19
    modeling of values by, 17–18
    partner-leaders, 15–19
Leadership and the Customer Revolution (Heil,
    Parker, and Tate), 170–171
Leadership Jazz (De Pree), 174
Leading Change (O'Toole), 135–136
Leading questions, in machine mentoring,
    162–163
Learning. *See also* Mentoring
    adult learning, 25–26
    axioms of, 25–26
    elements of learning plan, 147
    inside resources for, 170–171
    journal keeping and, 173
    judgment-free attitude for, 175
    mentoring and, xvii, 7–8
    out-of-the-way resources for, 172
    outside resources for, 171
    readiness for, 140
    reciprocal learning in peer mentoring, 117
    remote learning, 143–148
    resources for, 169–174
    self-directed learning method, 147
    teachable moment and, 124–125
Learning care packages for remote learning,
    145–146
Learning journal, 173
Learning organization, xi–xii
Learning plan, elements of, 148
Letting go, at end of mentoring, 167–168
Leveling communication, 51

Listening
    by leaders, 17
    focus and, 89
    importance of, 87–88
    mirroring and, 90–91
    and protégé's cues, 91–92
    reporter position for, 89–90
Little Prince, The (Saint-Exupéry), 174
Long-distance mentoring, 143–148
Love and Will (May), 134

Machine mentoring, 159–163
Managers. *See* Leadership; Mentoring "Mask
    removal," 84
May, Rollo, 134
Mentor Scale, 37–44, 72–73, 114–115, 126
Mentoring. *See also* Accepting; Expanding;
    Gifting; Learning; Surrendering
    advice and, 57–62
    affirmative action and, xvii, 6
    around equipment, 159–163
    associations with word, 5–6
    balance and, 123–129
    catalyst role in, 96
    definition of, x, 6
    dialogue and, 93–102
    end of, 165–168
    fear and, 103–110
    feedback and, 62–66
    follow-up on, 167–168
    history of term, 7–8
    hit-and-run approach to, 139–142
    learning and, xvii, 7–8
    listening and, 87–92
    magical quality of, x
    partnership and, 19
    partnership philosophy of, x–xi
    passionate connections and, 131–137
    peer mentoring, 111–118
    qualities of great mentoring partnerships,
        26–28
    questioning and, 67–75
    rapport in, 49–55
    remote learning and, 143–148
    resources on, 169–174
    role plays on, 153–158
    roles of mentors, 22–26
    SAGE as recipe for, 11–12
    self-assessment scale on, 37–44, 72–73,
        114–115, 126
    synchrony and synergy of, x
    traps to avoid in, 8–10
    trust and, 77–82
    white-water wisdom on, 139–142
Mind set, and dialogues, 94–95
Mirroring, and listening, 90–91

Mistakes, as opportunities to learn, 16–17
"Mockingbirds" (Oliver), 52–53
Modeling of values, by leaders, 17–18
Mohammed, 75
Moses, 75
Mother Teresa, 135
Motivator, as mentoring role, 23
Murray, W. H., 137
My Fair Lady, 110
Myers, Dee Dee, 80

Nadler, Leonard, 2, 147
Nanosecond Nineties, 139
NationsBank, 9, 167
Needs
    achievement need, 107
    control need, 108
    fear as threatened need, 106–108
    power need, 107
    recognition need, 107
Networking, and remote learning, 146–148
Nonverbal communication, 51, 99
Nordstrom, Bruce, 135
North Carolina National Bank, 9, 167
Nostalgia, 167

Odyssey, The (Homer), 7
Oliver, Mary, 52–53
Olmos, Edward James, 103–104
On Excellence (Gardner), 174
Openness
    balance and, 126
    inquiry talents and, 72–73
    in Mentor Scale, 43, 72–73, 115, 126
    in peer mentoring, 115
O'Toole, James, 135–136
Owner's Manual to the Brain, The (Howard), 70
Paper Chase, The, 103–104
Paraphrasing, in dialogues, 96–98
Parker, Tom, 170–171
Partner, as mentoring role, 24–25
Partner-leaders, 15–19
Partnership
    celebration and, 18–19
    encouragement of risk taking in employees,
        16–17
    keys to effectiveness in, 16–19
    listening and, 17
    and modeling of values, 17–18
    qualities of great mentoring partnerships,
        26–28
Passion
    boldness and, 136–137
    honesty of, 133–134
    importance of, 28
    as invitational, 134–136

Pedagogy versus andragogy, 25
Peer mentoring
    avoiding conditional affirmations in, 113, 116
    humility and, 112–113
    in Mentor Scale, 114–115
    questioning in, 113
    reciprocal learning in, 117
    resistance and, 113
    resistance in, 116–117
Perfection, avoidance of, 128–129
Performance problem or goal, in advice giving,
    58–59
Personality, as "mask," 49–50
Peters, Tom, xi, 139
Pirsig, Robert, 174
PKS Information Services, 132
"Playing over your head," 19
Powell, John, 84
Pride, 176
Protégés. See Mentoring
Pyramid relationships, 15

Questioning
    closed questions, 71, 74
    curiosity and, 74–75, 175–176
    for higher-level thinking, 71, 74
    human brain and, 69–70
    initiating and clarifying questions in, 96
    leading questions in machine mentoring,
        162–163
    in peer mentoring, 113
    Socratic teaching and, 67–68
    starting with setup statement, 70–71
    techniques for, 70–75
    "why" questions, 74

Ram Dass, x
Rapport
    components of, 50–53
    definition of, 50
    gifting gestures and, 51–52
    leveling communication and, 51
    receptivity for feelings in, 52–53
    reflective responses in, 53
Readiness for learning, 140
Receptivity for feelings, 52–53
Reciprocal learning, in peer mentoring, 117
Recognition need, 107
Reflective responses, in rapport building, 53
Remote learning
    buddy system for, 144–145
    elements of learning plan, 148
    learning care packages for, 145–146
    networking and, 146–148
    self-directed learning method, 147
Reporter position, for listening, 89–90

Rescuing versus support, 125, 127–128, 140–141
Resistance
    avoidance of, in advice giving, 58–60
    on not resisting resistance, 116–117
    in peer mentoring, 113, 116–117
Restatement, in paraphrasing, 96–97
Restatement in opposite terms, in paraphrasing, 97
Risk taking, encouragement of, in employees, 16–17
Ritz Carlton, 135
Roberts, Julia, 133
Rogers, Carl, 11, 52
Role plays
    allowing drag time in, 156
    feedback on, 156–157
    practice, feedback, practice in, 157
    reasons people don't like, 153–154
    review, renew, refine in, 157–158
    setup for, 154–156
Roles of mentors, 22–26
Royal Dutch/Shell, xi

SAGE, 11–12
Saint-Exupéry, Antoine de, 174
Scale on mentoring, 37–44, 72–73, 114–115, 126
Schulze, Horst, 135
Schutz, Will, 42
Schweitzer, Albert, 135
Scottish Himalayan Expedition, The (Murray), 137
Self-assessment mentoring scale, 37–44, 72–73, 114–115, 126
Self-directed learning method, 148
Self-esteem, fear and, 109–110
Sellers, Patricia, 52
Senge, Peter, xi
Sergeant, as mentoring role, 24
Seuss, Dr., 170
Sitting-on-the-right actions, 79–80
Smith, Larry, 131–133
Sociability
    balance and, 126
    inquiry talents and, 72
    in Mentor Scale, 42, 72, 114, 126
    in peer mentoring, 114
Socratic method, 67–75, 96
Southwest Airlines, 135
Specific to general paraphrasing, 97
Speed, 139–142
Stand and Deliver, 103–104
Steel Magnolias, 133
Summarizing, in dialogues, 98
Supervisors. See Leadership; Mentoring

Support without rescuing, 125, 127–128, 140–141
Surrendering
    advice and, 57–62
    definition of, 46
    effectiveness of, 47
    in The Empire Strikes Back, 46
    feedback and, 62–66
    in mentoring, 11
    questioning and, 67–75
    rapport and, 49–55
    trust and, 77–82
Swift, Jonathan, 150
Sympathy, versus empathy, 53
Synthesis, and questioning, 71

Tate, Rick, 170–171
Teachable moment, 124–125
Time
    and hit-and-run approach to mentoring, 139–142
    for learner readiness, 140
    for support, not rescuing, 140–141
Transparent Self, The (Jourard), 84
Traps to avoid in mentoring, 8–10
Trust
    and clean communication, 65
    and communication of competence, 81–82
    definition of, 81
    humility and, 80–81
    importance of, 27
    and sitting-on-the-right actions, 79–80
Truth. See Honesty
Tway, Duane, 81

Unconditional positive regard, 11, 52

Vaill, Peter, xi
Values, modeling of, by leaders, 17–18

Walton, Sam, 135
Waterman, Bob, xi
Wayne, John, 156
"White water" metaphor, xi
White-water wisdom, 139–142
Who's Afraid of Virginia Woolf? (Albee), 94
Why Am I Afraid to Tell You Who I Am? (Powell), 84
"Why" questions, 74
Wizard, as mentoring role, 22

Zemke, Ron, 117, 136
Zen and the Art of Motorcycle Maintenance (Pirsig), 174

ABOUT THE AUTHOR

CHIP R. BELL is a senior partner with Performance Research Associates, Inc., and manages its Dallas office. PRA consults with organizations on ways they can build long-term customer loyalty. He has served as consultant or trainer to such major organizations as IBM, GE, Microsoft, AT&T, Motorola, Marriott, Victoria's Secret, 3M, GTE, Shell Oil, Eli Lilly, First Union, CompuServe, and Cadillac. Before starting a consulting firm in the late 1970s, he was vice president and director of management and organization development for NCNB Corporation (now NationsBank). He was an infantry-unit commander with the 82nd Airborne Division in Vietnam and in 1970 served on the staff of the Instructional Methods Division of the U.S. Army Infantry School.

While his most recent best-selling books have focused on service quality (*Customers As Partners* and, with consulting partner Ron Zemke, *Managing Knock Your Socks Off Service*), Dr. Bell is the author or coauthor of *Instructing for Results, Understanding Training, The Trainer's Professional Development Handbook,* and *Clients and Consultants.* He has also contributed chapters to *The Sales Training Handbook, The Training and Development Handbook,* and *The Handbook of Human Resource Development.*

His articles on training and learning have appeared in such professional journals as *Training and Development, Training, HR Magazine, Educational Leadership, Adult Training, Storyteller's Journal,* and the *Journal of Management Development* (UK). Chip's articles on leadership and mentoring have appeared in *Management Review, Supervisory Management, Advanced Management Journal, Executive Excellence, Executive Directions, Quality Digest,* and *Today's Leaders.* He currently serves on the editorial advisory board of *Training and Development,* the professional journal of the American Society for Training and Development.

Chip R. Bell
Performance Research Associates, Inc.
25 Highland Park #100
Dallas, Texas 75205-2785
Phone: (214) 522-5777
Fax: (214) 691-7591
E-mail: PRAWest@AOL.COM

Berrett-Koehler Publishers

BERRETT-KOEHLER is an independent publisher of books, periodicals, and other publications at the leading edge of new thinking and innovative practice on work, business, management, leadership, stewardship, career development, human resources, entrepreneurship, and global sustainability.

Since the company's founding in 1992, we have been committed to supporting the movement toward a more enlightened world of work by publishing books, periodicals, and other publications that help us to integrate our values with our work and work lives, and to create more humane and effective organizations.

We have chosen to focus on the areas of work, business, and organizations, because these are central elements in many people's lives today. Furthermore, the work world is going through tumultuous changes, from the decline of job security to the rise of new structures for organizing people and work. We believe that change is needed at all levels—individual, organizational, community, and global—and our publications address each of these levels.

We seek to create new lenses for understanding organizations, to legitimize topics that people care deeply about but that current business orthodoxy censors or considers secondary to bottom-line concerns, and to uncover new meaning, means, and ends for our work and work lives.

See next page for other books from Berrett-Koehler Publishers

Other leading-edge business books from Berrett-Koehler Publishers

Dance Lessons

Six Steps to Great Partnerships in Business and Life

Chip R. Bell and Heather Shea

DANCE LESSONS is a comprehensive guide to the interpersonal side of partnerships, revealing exactly how the champions choreograph their partnership dances for show-stopping performances. Bell and Shea offer an in-depth look at how we can successfully manage partnerships and build them with substance—passion, quality, heart, and soul—and show how to develop meaningful, ethical, and soulful partnerships in every interaction in your work and your life.

Hardcover, 200 pages, 10/98 • ISBN 1-57675-043-4 CIP • **Item no. 50434-258 $24.95**

Audiotape, 2 cassettes/3 hours • ISBN 1-5651-1272-5 • **Item no. 12725-258 $17.95**

Customers As Partners

Building Relationships That Last

Chip R. Bell

WRITTEN WITH PASSION and humor, this groundbreaking work provides step-by-step guidelines for enhancing long-term customer loyalty and achieving lasting success. Chip Bell offers insights on how to keep the quality of customer relationships central in every interaction by creating sustaining personal bonds—the true source of profitability.

Paperback, 256 pages, 1/96 • ISBN 1-881052-78-8 CIP **Item no. 52788-258 $15.95**

Hardcover 9/94 • ISBN 1-881052-54-0 CIP **Item no. 52540-258 $24.95**

Managers As Facilitators

A Practical Guide to Getting Work Done in a Changing Workplace

Richard G. Weaver and John D. Farrell

MANAGERS AS FACILITATORS details a practical, effective program to help transform leaders and managers in all types of organizations into skilled facilitators, providing them with the skills and tools they need to create the changes they want in their organizations.

Hardcover, 250 pages, 5/97 • ISBN 1-57675-016-7 CIP **Item no. 50167-258 $27.95**

Available at your favorite bookstore, or call (800) 929-2929

Empowerment Takes More than a Minute

Ken Blanchard, John Carlos, and Alan Randolph

EMPOWERMENT TAKES MORE THAN A MINUTE is the book that finally goes beyond the empowerment rhetoric to show managers how to achieve true, lasting results in their organizations. These expert authors explain how to empower the workforce by moving from a command-and-control mindset to a supportive, responsibility-centered environment in which all employees have the opportunity and responsibility to do their best. They explain how to build ownership and trust using three essential keys to making empowerment work in large and small organizations.

Hardcover, 140 pages, 12/96 • ISBN 1-881052-83-4 CIP
Item no. 52834-258 $20.00

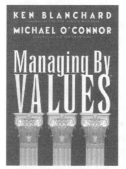

Managing By Values

Ken Blanchard and Michael O'Connor

BASED ON over twenty-five years of research and application, *Managing by Values* provides a practical game plan for defining, clarifying, and communicating an organization's values and insuring that it's practices are in line with those values.

Hardcover, 140 pages, 1/97 • ISBN 1-57675-007-8 CIP
Item no. 50078-258 $20.00

The Age of Participation
New Governance for the Workplace and the World

by Patricia McLagan and Christo Nel
foreword by Peter Block

PATRICIA MCLAGAN and Christo Nel describe the massive transformation that is occurring in human institutions today. Blending theory and practice, providing numerous examples, and drawing on more than forty years of experience in over 200 organizations, McLagan and Nel describe what executives, managers, workers, labor unions, customers, and suppliers can do as part of a participative enterprise. In this practical, experience-based handbook, they look closely at every level of life in a participative organization and deflate the fears and misperceptions that can sabotage change.

Paperback, 340 pages, 1/97 • ISBN 1-56765-012-4 CIP **Item no. 50124-258 $18.95**
Hardcover, 9/95 • ISBN 1-881052-56-7 CIP **Item no. 52567-258 $27.95**

Available at your favorite bookstore, or call (800) 929-2929

A Higher Standard of Leadership
Lessons from the Life of Gandhi

Keshavan Nair

THIS IS THE FIRST BOOK to apply lessons from Gandhi's life to the practical tasks faced by today's business and political leaders. Through illustrative examples from Gandhi's life and writings, Keshavan Nair explores the process of making decisions, setting goals, and implementing actions in the spirit of service that is essential to the realization of a higher standard of leadership in our workplaces and communities.

Paperback, 174 pages, 1/97 • ISBN 1-57675-011-6 CIP
Item no. 50116-258 $16.95

The Courageous Follower
Standing Up To and For Our Leaders

Ira Chaleff

LEADERS CANNOT EXIST without followers. Every great leader must, therefore, be surrounded by great followers. At last, here is a book to balance the hundreds of management books on leadership, which gives followers the insights and tools necessary to partner effectively with their leaders. For anyone who works closely with a leader of any kind, this is a comprehensive guide for positively influencing that relationship and helping the leader use power wisely to accomplish the organization's purpose. It is a handbook that readers can refer to repeatedly when confronted with the challenges of supporting and, at times, correcting a leader.

Hardcover, 280 pages, 6/95 • ISBN 1-881052-66-4 CIP **Item no. 52664-258 $24.95**

On Our Own Terms
Portraits of Women Business Leaders

Liane Enkelis and Karen Olsen, with Marion Lewenstein
Foreword by Jane Applegate

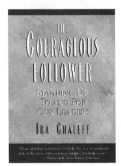

FIFTEEN WOMEN CEOs and presidents of companies with annual revenues of $10 million or more tell how they got to the top —on their terms. Through personal interviews and striking photographs these business leaders reveal how they broke through the gender barrier to achieve top executive positions, and how they learned to balance family needs with work responsibilities.

Paperback original, 168 pages, 10/95 • ISBN 1-881052-69-9 CIP
Item no. 52699-258 $19.95

Available at your favorite bookstore, or call (800) 929-2929